The High Legal Road

A New Approach to Legal Problems

Sloan Bashinsky, J.D.

The High
Legal Road

Library of Congress Catalog Card Number: 90-080871
ISBN: 0-929077-99-7

Essential Publications
Post Office Box 101555
Birmingham, Alabama 35210

The High Legal Road

A New Approach to Legal Problems

by Sloan Bashinsky, J.D.

Essential Publications
Birmingham, Alabama

Acknowledgements

Many people have been catalysts for me during the last few years. I will not name them here, but I will say they had various backgrounds and beliefs. They never came when I expected them. They never gave what I expected them to give. They never said what I wanted to hear. Yet each of them appeared at the right time giving and saying just the right thing. And they all loved me. At times I doubted their love because they pushed me to face myself and do things I did not want to do. And they taught me to laugh instead of cry. To all of my teachers, I give my deep appreciation and love.

Contents

To my son who died generously.

Opening Remarks

This book represents a significant departure from my earlier books' saucy but serious treatments of buying and selling a home and the lawyer-client relationship. Although those books were criticized by Realtors and lawyers, I had fun writing them, and enjoyed being interviewed by consumer journals, the press, and appearing on radio and television—especially the ego-gratifying appearances on NBC's *Today*, *The CBS Morning News*, and CNN. But mainly, I was satisfied to have helped a few people survive in a complex legal system. People still call me to say those books were important—that they changed their lives.

That said, there is something about my earlier books I wish to say. It concerns a theme central to this book. Those books were cast within the legal adversarial framework. While legal fighting may ensure survival, it prevents peaceful living and healing. This book takes a giant leap. It presents a radical idea: that is, jumping entirely out of legal battles by using legal problems as opportunities for spiritual healing.

Shamanistic healers view their patients' illnesses as windows into the spiritual realms, and thus as windows to healing. The clergy often take a similar approach to their parishioners' personal troubles. The Swiss psychiatrist, C.G. (Carl) Jung, often used this concept to solve the riddle of psychological and physical illness. More recently, M. Scott Peck, Bernie Siegel, Stephen Levine, and many others have written about helping patients and clients use psychological and physical dis-ease as an opportunity to heal spiritual emptiness. So these concepts are not new, but my application of them to legal problems is.

Certainly, this is not the sort of book one would expect from a University of Alabama School of Law graduate, yet the seed may well have been planted by my law professor, Dr. Sam Beatty, who said, "Next to the ministry, being a lawyer is the most difficult calling in the world." That was one of the few practical things I was taught about being a lawyer, for when I graduated I held an unrealistic idealism toward my profession: I envisioned myself charging forth as my clients' champion, righting wrongs, and achieving justice.

That rose-colored view did not last. I realized after opening my practice in 1972 that Dr. Beatty was right. My clients brought me almost every kind of human tragedy: divorce and child custody fights; spouse and child abuse; alcoholism; drug addiction; crime; death of or injury to a loved one; bankruptcy; and being sued. They suffered deeply, and I was powerless to help them. They wanted me to do something to "the other side" to make their lives better. They seldom took responsibility for their sorrows. Regardless of whether they won or lost, they harbored bitterness towards the other side, judge and jury, and sometimes even me long after their case was over. It is fair to say most of those clients will take their hatred to their graves.

Of course, I also had good experiences with clients. I was often able to save them much grief, and many of

them were grateful. Yet too many of them were emotionally and spiritually destroyed by their cases. My lawyer
friends say they have had many similar experiences with
their clients. While many lawyers thrive in this type of
environment, an equal number do not, and experience
physical and psychological complaints, alcoholism,
narcotics addiction, divorce, and law firm break-ups as
a result of the stress generated in the practice of law.

I remember one day in late 1983, when I ate lunch with
two lawyer friends, swapping a few stories about our
clients, cases, and other lawyers. Something was said that
caused me to complain about what a pain in the neck
clients could be. Sitting at a near-by table was a slim,
gray-haired lawyer I admire. He walked past our table
on his way out, and asked me to drop by for a visit.
About two weeks later, I went to see him. I sat down
in the chair beside his plain desk in his old-fashioned
office. He had never taken to fancy furnishings, preferring
to spend his money on his law library and family. The
gleam in his eyes belied his eighty-three years. He looked
me straight in the eye and said, "Sloan, I think what you
need to do to be happy is find God. That's all I wanted
to say to you." I blinked, flushed, sputtered, clumsily
thanked him, and left. I knew he was right, but did not
have a clue as to how to find God, for I had felt estranged
from my Creator all my life.

A year later, I decided I was not suited to be a lawyer,
and wound down my law practice. By Thanksgiving of
1985, I had transferred my clients to other lawyers. I
"dropped out" and moved to Santa Fe where I had heard
God lived, albeit not by that name. Many people thought
I was nuts; some said they understood; and a few (some
of whom were lawyers) confided then that they envied
me. During my search, I met many people who told me

the answers were in me. Yet stubbornly I hoped to find my answers "out there"—that there was a magic pill or enlightened master waiting for me just around the next bend in the road.

Slowly, I realized my teachers were right—that the solutions I sought were in me. Only then did I begin to make progress. There were many hard lessons in which my ego was "adjusted." That is, I was required to face things in myself I despised, some of which I share in this book. And there were many mystical encounters with "Spirit." (I use the word, Spirit, in the context of mystical experiences, instead of God, because I never know whether or not God, an angel or some other spirit being, or my soul is behind these experiences. When I make direct reference to my Creator, I simply say God.) One such mystical experience led me to write this book, and I will share it with you now, and a few others I will share later.

One fall day in 1987, I drove along the Arkansas River through the majestic Sangre de Cristo mountains in southern Colorado. The Indians and Spanish descendents believe these 14,000 feet high peaks contain magic, as the translation,"the blood of Christ," implies. As I admired the beauty of these towering mountains, it dawned on me that I would soon return to the law and would write another book about it. I was surprised, because I thought I was finished with both the law and writing. I knew I would watch with interest for what unfolded.

I returned to Boulder, where I then lived, had dinner, and went to bed. I woke at 3 a.m. and could not go back to sleep. I often wake at this time of night, and I usually welcome it. It is a time when I receive most of my intuitive knowledge, and it is when spiritual teachers say we are most open to the spiritual energies. Nevertheless, I was annoyed, because I was to begin an intensive training at the Hakomi Institute in Boulder at 9 a.m. that morning. (Hakomi is a form of psychotherapy; the name is borrowed from an ancient Hopi Indian word, meaning: "How do I stand in these many realms?") I lived alone at the time, and complained to whomever or whatever might be listening, "I don't need this; I need to sleep!"

A voice just above me, yet in my room, answered, "Get up and begin the book." I was startled and said nothing.

Again the voice, "Get up and start the book."

"No way!" I said angrily, "I need to sleep!"

"Start now!" the voice insisted.

"Why now? Why not tomorrow night?" I begged.

"Now!" the voice commanded.

"Right this very minute?" My shoulders sagged.

"Yes," it said.

So I got up and began the introduction to a book for which I had no material. I proceeded assuming I had been appointed "legal messiah." Although that egotistical notion provided stimulus to write the book, it also led to many painful lessons about arrogance.

I finished the Hakomi training and moved back to Birmingham. Then, people who had read my earlier books began calling for help with their legal problems. My law license was inactive, so I could not act as their lawyer, which I did not want to do anyway. I had been taught by John Upledger, D.O. of Palm Beach Gardens, Florida, how to help people decode the symbolic messages in dreams and illness, through which we are often taught when we are not living as we should. I sensed legal difficulties could also be solved this way, and invited these early "clients" (a few were lawyers) to join me in an experiment to test this theory, and hopefully provide supporting material for this book, which was going nowhere fast.

Together we found in my "mystical" legal laboratory that there was far more to our legal problems than met the eye: they were major intersections in our lives and embodied many spiritual lessons. In every case, we found we had done something to set in motion events which culminated in our legal woes. No cases, no matter how horrible, were mere accidents, quirks of fate, or all somebody else's fault. Try as we might, we were unable to wriggle out of having at least co-created our legal woes. We realized our cases proved the spiritual law of cause and effect: that we had reaped what we had unwittingly sown.

When we saw how we had co-created our own legal messes, we were mortified. We were even more mortified to discover that, if we did not do something to correct what we had done to set up our legal problems, then something else awful later happend to get our attention: illness, physical injury, relationship upheaval, emotional disturbance, business reversal, death of someone dear to us, etc. Almost always, our lives got worse if we missed the spiritual lessons, and the reverse was also true: our lives got better if we learned the lessons.

If you find yourself uncomfortable reading this, then you are having a normal response. My clients and I had the same reaction when we first discovered these things. We wanted to blame our legal difficulties on chance, fate, others, or God. Taking responsibility for having co-created them was the next-to-last thing we wanted to do. The last thing we wanted to do was correct the behavior which set up our legal problems. Yet we saw that if we did not do that, we would get another chance to learn our lessons. There was no way to avoid the lessons: we could only choose to avoid learning them.

When we came to understand and appreciate what I have just shared with you, most (but not all) of us chose to take a very different approach to our cases than we otherwise would have taken. Instead of seeking revenge, "justice," or a lot of money, we concentrated on knowing and changing ourselves so we would not set ourselves up for another bad experience. We got our own houses in order, before attempting to put our legal adversaries' houses in order. We sought healing instead of revenge— fair compensation, rather than a jack-pot money verdict. As a result, we experienced healing in many areas of our lives. This theme is expanded in Chapters 1-5.

Related to this is the false view many have of justice in this country. All too many people equate justice with punishment, revenge, proving who's right, etc. People who seek such such "justice" usually seek it to avoid imposing true justice on themselves. They think they are right and all who disagree with them are wrong. They seek the truth only insofar as it supports their position. They are not interested in "the truth, the whole truth, and nothing but the truth." They are not interested in seeing how they commit in their own hearts and in other areas of their lives the very crimes they seek to punish others for. I address these matters more fully in Chapter six.

There is much for lawyers to see, too. Their own spiritual lessons are mirrored to them by their clients' cases. I share with you throughout the book how my clients have mirrored my own lessons, and in Chapter 7 you will read about how other lawyers were similarly mirrored by their clients.

On a broader scale, the legal profession has experienced dissatisfaction with the practice of law within its own ranks. Many lawyers suffer "burn out." They hit the saloons and go-go bars after work, use drugs, run around on their wives, are lifeless at home, over-bill their clients, take in fees and then do nothing, and mishandle cases. The profession ranks very low in public opinion polls, and legal malpractice suits are on the rise.

The Bar is aware of these problems, and would like to do something about them. So far, its efforts to halt the legal slide have been ineffective. This is because the Bar has focused on eliminating symptoms. It needs to look deeper. It needs to see the lessons beyond the symptoms. Then it can act on the lessons. Otherwise, the symptoms will simply get worse. Legislative efforts to curb lawyers will increase. Legal malpractice suits will become as popular as medical malpractice suits. Instead of being ranked with doctors, real estate agents, and used car dealers in public opinion polls, lawyers may gain a special ranking at the bottom of the social ladder. I offer suggestions in Chapter 7 about how the Bar can avert this diminished status.

Similar lessons are presented to society, and similar opportunities for healing are also available to it. More wives and children are injured and killed in domestic violence than in automobile accidents; many fathers have sex with their daughters; millions of children run in gangs, take alcohol, legal and illegal drugs, dress weirdly, and commit suicide; our inner cities crumble under the weight of poverty, crime and drugs; crime is epidemic throughout our country, and is at its worst in Washington, D.C., where our nation's lawmakers are; the environment is being destroyed; race discrimination is nearly as great as it was when George Wallace blocked the doors at the University of Alabama; Satanism, Nazism, and other reactionary cults are gaining strength; the National Rifle Association is our most powerful political lobby and the best friend the drug dealers have, next to the American chemical companies which supply ninety-five percent of the chemicals needed to process cocaine; health care and weaponry are our biggest industries (an interesting combination); our national economy is in shambles.

These terrible problems have resulted from our suppressing the symptoms, instead of probing for the root causes and doing something about them. We prefer to kill the messenger. In killing the messenger, we set ourselves up for harder lessons which will come in the not-too-distant future. We need to take a different approach. We need to view our collective lawlessness as a symptom of a deeper imbalance. We must deal with the root causes and learn our collective spiritual lessons. The symptoms will then be easier to treat. I address these concerns more fully in Chapter 8.

The "case/analysis" method is used to teach law students, and I use that method in this book. Numerous cases are used to demonstrate the high legal road approach to solving legal disputes. Names and a few facts in the cases about other people have been changed to protect them, however nothing essential has been omitted. Due to the large number of cases used and the importance of each case to the points I make, you might find this book reads easier in small bits, a chapter every day or so. Then go back and read it straight through. Or you might want to read the book straight through, then re-read a chapter every day or so. Either approach will, I think, make the book more meaningful and useful to you than a single reading.

I have read dozens of books on healing. Some were more helpful than others. The most helpful (for me) were books which revealed the authors as people—books in which the authors got down in the trenches and walked beside me. I trust and feel safe with those who show me the way by their own example, and I use that approach in this book.

In addition to the cases and my analysis of them, there are challenging exercises for you to do that will also help you discover the truth which is often difficult to face but without which healing is impossible. You may resist doing some of these exersises, and I invite you to ponder your resistance. Remember, the ego fears the truth, but the soul thirsts for it. That is why Jesus said, "Seek to know the truth and the truth shall make you free."

I find universal wisdom in Jesus's essential teachings, wisdom as applicable to legal problems as to any other problems, and I use Jesus's essential teachings in my work and in this book. That said, this book is not about Jesus, nor does it intend to promote Christianity. In fact, I find many "Christians" tend to misinterpret Jesus's teachings and thus misapply his teachings in their legal affairs. I think the misuse of Jesus's teachings is one of the root causes of our individual and collective legal woes.

This book is controversial: it may challenge your beliefs, cause you to feel uncomfortable, and make you angry. You may want to throw it away before you finish reading it. You may want to write me and tell me off, or tell me I don't know what I'm talking about. I do not claim to have all the answers. Being human, I cannot know all there is to know, anymore than can you. I have had certain unusual experiences and insights which I share here and which I invite you to consider rather than either blindly accept or reject out of hand.

As you read this book, pretend you are a skeptical juror hearing a case on a subject you know nothing about. Please hold your decision until all evidence is in. Separate the wheat from the chaff, the substance from the form, the real from the illusion. Weigh the arguments of your ego against the yearning of your soul. As you do so, remember that your ego tells you what you want to hear, while your soul tells you what you need to hear, which is seldom what you want to hear. Make your decision based on the truth, the whole truth, and nothing but the truth, then take whatever action you deem appropriate. Thank you, and now I will present my case for the high legal road.

Chapter One

Big Picture Law

Traditional medicine treats most illness symptomatically. The physical complaints may be removed or suppressed, but the underlying causes often remain and continue to create problems for patients, as evidenced by the large number of people suffering today from chronic illnesses. In fact, doctor friends tell me that medicine and surgery heal only about five percent of medical patients—that the remaining ninety-five percent get well on their own, stay chronically sick, or die.

Quite a few doctors are beginning to take a more complete approach to medicine by inviting patients to explore and work with the personal lessons symbolically mirrored by their illness. For instance, a problem in the area of the mouth or throat metaphorically suggests an inability to say what's on one's mind, to say what one feels, to be one's true self. In such a case, the doctor encourages a patient to learn to be real and thus cure the underlying cause of the illness.

The most well-known of these remarkable doctors may be Bernie Siegel, M.D., author of *Love, Medicine, and Miracles* and *Peace, Love, and Healing*. Dr. Siegel, a cancer surgeon and a professor at Yale Medical School, is not against drugs and surgery, but he advocates that his patients not solely rely on them. He finds drugs and surgery tend to get much better results *after* his patients probe into, decode, and do something about the deeper meaning (the root causes) of their disease.

You may wonder what this has to do with legal problems. Well, lawyers are legal doctors: they treat legal rather than medical disease, and use negotiating and the court room rather than drugs and the operating room. As in medicine, about five percent of legal clients respond well to the traditional symptomatic treatment: negotiating and court battles. In the other ninety-five percent of cases, the legal problem—the symptom—may be removed, but the underlying causes continue to fester and plague clients. Witness how cases escalate, the physical and psychological stress they cause, and the emotional breakdown and illness which often occur *after* it is all over.

Legal cases, like illnesses, have deeper causes and resolve more favorably when the underlying dynamics are explored and worked through *before the outer symptoms are treated*. I have found this to be true in all cases, regardless of the client's religious or spiritual persuasion, and I have worked with people of many faiths and beliefs: Christians, Catholics, Jews, Buddhists, Sufis, New Agers, agnostics, and atheists. That said, let's look at cases in point. I begin with the major case in my own life.

My Son's Death

My son was born when I was a senior in law school. Soon after his birth, his mother, Dianne, and I traveled around to show him off to various friends and relatives. On the way back from our trip, we decided traveling with him was not a good idea, and not to travel with him again until he was several months old. When we got home, Dianne's brother called from their parents' home in Memphis, where we had just been, to say he was passing through before going overseas with the Air Force. Dianne said she was going back to Memphis, and began to pack. I reminded her of our agreement, and she said she was going anyway. I got mad, and we had a terrible argument. I drove her and our baby to the airport, arguing violently all the way. They got on the airplane, and I never saw my son again. He died two days later of Sudden Infant Death Syndrome (SIDS).

The Memphis police department made a homicide investigation which was reported in my home town newspapers. I wrote angry letters to the editor and gave serious thought to filing a lawsuit for libel and invasion of privacy. Fortunately, the lawyer I consulted wisely advised me against that course of action. "Regardless of the merits of your case, the emotional stress it would generate would destroy you and your wife," he said. This happened over twenty years ago, before I understood the ways of Spirit. I did not see the curious progression—the agreement, the argument, my son's death, and the homicide investigation—until I was in the middle of writing this book. When I saw it, I became distraught to think I had murdered my son.

This incident was what I call a "waking dream," an outer event mirroring my inner reality—my relationship with my internalized parents, myself, and God. More specifically, my father's world was the world of intellect and business; my mother's was the world of feelings and religion. They fought, mostly covertly, over my destiny, each fearing the other's world, both believing they did the right thing. Their fight created a deep split in me that separated me from my true self, and caused me to doubt a God that would give me such parents. I played out that split by fighting with Dianne and by unwittingly trying to bequeath it to my son, whose soul declined that inheritance and chose to leave instead. In leaving, he blasted me out of both my parents' worlds, and started me on a search for myself.

My search was greatly retarded by my inability to see the deepest lesson in this experience—reconnecting with God, both within and without. I knew unconditional love with my son, something I had not previously experienced. When he died, taking that love with him, I felt like a huge, back hole had been gouged in me. The hole was my separation from God, a separation I had not before felt. Instead of paying attention to my feelings and doing something about what they revealed, I hated myself for not standing up to Dianne, blamed God for my son's death, and enlarged the hole.

Twenty years passed before I allowed myself to step back and look at my son's death from a spiritual perspective. When I finally did that, I shook all over and cried like a baby. I felt I would die—that I was in a ten-point Richter-scale, emotional earthquake, which is how coming face-to-face with a long-avoided spiritual lesson usually affects you. This experience is metaphorically described in the 23rd Psalm as walking "through the valley of the shadow of death," a place I call "the shaky zone."

When you are in the shaky zone, eye-to-eye with the truth, you fear you will be destroyed, and most of us do whatever we can to make that terror go away: we file a lawsuit, get other people to comfort us, and engage in addictive or compulsive behavior. But if we hang in there without trying to reduce the heat, and allow the experience to wash through us, we are not destroyed. Rather we walk beside God and emerge stronger for having done that. And, in fact, that happened for me.

After allowing myself to see the painful truth about my son's death—that it was not God's fault, an accident, or a quirk of faith, I became stronger and was then able to begin healing the split in myself and my separation from God.

Now let's look at cases involving other people, some of whom entered the valley of the shadow of death, and some of whom did not.

The Buddhist

Valerie, a woman in her late twenties, came to me with many problems surrounding her marriage, her previous marriage, and the children of both marriages. She practiced Tibetan Buddhism. I said if we were going to work together, we should work on the spiritual aspects of her case as well as her other concerns.

"I feel comfortable with my spiritual life," she said, "I need help with my legal problems."

"Are you at peace within yourself?" I asked. She looked suspiciously at me.

"You do not seem to be at peace," I said, "and if we are going to work together, we are going to explore why you are so miserable."

Valerie began to squirm. She was uncomfortable because I challenged the effectiveness of her spiritual practices. After some sparring, she did agree to continue the session. As we worked, she saw beneath her Buddhism a deeper childhood belief in a punishing *male* God. She saw the connection between her image of God and her overly critical, God-fearing father, who symbolized God to her when she was very young. She saw how her problems with her husbands were linked to her childhood experiences with her father and with her childhood image of a punishing, male God. Although her Buddhism had helped her in many ways, it had not healed her problems with God, problems which were at the core of her marital problems. Valerie became distraught: she wanted to be a Buddhist and never have to deal with "God" again. She left, and I do not know how she resolved the matter because she never made another appointment. This often happens—clients not coming back—when they come face-to-face with that which they do not want to see.

I work with many people like Valerie whose childhood experiences separated them from God. They felt something was missing and adopted Eastern or New Age spiritual practices. While many of those practices are paths to God, if used correctly, most people I know who use them do so to avoid the initial spiritual wound. That wound cannot be healed by running away from it, or masking it with new beliefs. It can only be healed by turning and facing it: as some Buddhists would say, "by facing the dragon." The dragon guards the gate to heaven, and you cannot pass through the gate without dealing with the dragon. Now let's look at another case in which a client did not want to see his *real* legal adversary.

Father Knows Best

A man called from Kansas after reading my third book, *Kill All the Lawyers?*. He claimed he had been swindled in a land deal, and lost a great deal of money. He had filed a multi-million dollar lawsuit against several wealthy developers in his community. He looked forward to the sweet taste of revenge, and was anxious to come to Boulder and talk with me. I suggested we talk first on the telephone, as he might not want to work with me after hearing how I practiced law.

I explained how I viewed a legal wrangle as a small piece of a much bigger puzzle—as a metaphor for an unresolved internal wrangle. He said he did not understand. So I asked if he went to church, and he said he did—that he was Lutheran. I asked, had he heard the phrase, "The Lord works in mysterious ways?" He answered that he had.

"Well I think your case is about your relationship with God," I said.

There was a long silence, then he asked, "How old are you, young man?"

"Forty-six," I answered.

"Well, I'm seventy-six!"

And so it went. He was determined to prove I did not have enough years behind me to talk to him about God, even though he thought I was old enough to give him legal advice about a multi-million dollar lawsuit! The last thing this man wanted to do was take a broader view of his case. He was too intent on getting revenge and making a lot of money, to do that.

Let's unravel the symbolism in this case to see what was his big picture. There isn't much information, but there is enough to make an educated guess. Try to figure it out on your own, before you read my guess. Don't worry about getting it right. It takes a little time to learn how to do this.

What jumps out for me are four things: (1) his patronizing approach with me; (2) his efforts to make millions in a business deal; (3) his being swindled; and (4) his anger. Here's how I interpret those clues.

His patronizing approach struck me as a defense. I think if he were truly comfortable with his beliefs, then he would have been curious about my work. His greed for millions of dollars, far more than he needed to live comfortably, suggested he did not have inner wealth— a true connection with God. Otherwise, he would not have reacted so strongly to the loss. His hatred for the developers who swindled him reflected his own self-hatred for swindling himself of his inner wealth. The loss of a lot of money was, for him, somewhat like the loss of my son was for me. Both losses revealed the deep, black hole in us. I think the big picture for this man was to truly connect with God. Here's a similar case.

Fool's Gold

Roger was eager to share with me his "born again" experience and convert me to his faith, and was equally talkative about the bitter lawsuit he had filed against his business partner. He said his partner had cheated him out of a large percentage of his interest in their gold-mining partnership. I asked how he reconciled the lawsuit with Jesus's counsel against suing people. He said, "Jesus was against suing brothers in the faith, not unbelievers. I now see my partner is not really a Christian, so it's okay to sue him." I invited Roger to take a bigger view of his case, but he was closed to doing that. He was absolutely convinced he was correct—that God was on his side.

So what was Roger's big picture? Take a moment to see if you can figure it out before reading further.

What strikes me are: (1) Roger's fundamentalism; (2) his misapplication of Jesus's teachings; (3) his quest for gold; and (4) his feeling cheated. If I use these facts as symbolic clues, they reveal Roger's big picture. Here's how I decode these clues.

Roger hated his partner, judged him un-Christian, and sued him. Jesus said we should forgive our enemies, turn the other cheek, and give our coat to anyone who asks for it. He said we should not judge others unless we wish to be judged ourselves. He advised against lawsuits. Roger disregarded every one of these teachings, which indicated he was not really a follower of Jesus.

Another piece of evidence was his forceful proselytizing. I wondered why he did that if he really felt saved? Jesus never forced his views down other people's throats, and he advised his disciples not to do that either. That was another principle Jesus taught, one also rejected by Roger. My hunch is, Roger proselytized to compensate for the way he trampled Jesus's teachings, not just in this case, but in all his worldly relationships. He thought he could avoid the consequences of that behavior by saving other people—that he could "buy" his way into heaven with souls.

I think Roger yearned for the true gold, God. The gold mining business and the lawsuit reflected that. Gold symbolizes the ultimate *inner* goal of the spiritual seeker. Roger compensated for his lack of inner gold by seeking elemental gold, the most precious worldly metal. His loss of earthly gold triggered his deeper loss of inner gold. His hatred of his partner who cheated him, mirrored his hatred of himself for cheating himself out of inner gold.

Roger did not see *his* big picture. No doubt, his partner

had a similar big picture. Neither of them will see the big picture as long as they fight over "fool's" gold. Now let's look at other types of big-picture cases.

Unlucky In Love

Tim went through a string of divorces. In the first divorce, his wife made off with most of the money, the dogs, the car, and he got the bills and the mortgage payments on their low-equity home where he decided to stay. As the song goes, "She got the money, I got the shaft!" In the second divorce, his wife made off with their son by moving out of state. Before the third divorce, his wife became violent, throwing heavy objects like skillets and hammers at him. He moved out when she was away on vacation, fearing for his life if he moved out when she was home. Tim developed a chauvinistic philosophy of women, summed up by three rules he gleefully quotes to his men friends whenever they have women problems:

1. All women are crazy.

2. There is nothing that can be done to change them.

3. Never forget rules 1 and 2.

Tim now spends his leisure time hunting, working out, and hanging out in saloons. He never sees his son, and swears he will never marry again. So what do you think is his big picture? If you think it is about resolving his hatred of women, you are right. His hatred of women acted like a magnet for women who hate men and came back to haunt him. He reaped what he sowed by thought, word, and deed. That is the law of cause and effect so often taught by Jesus and other spiritual teachers. That law is used to teach us about ourselves.

To change this unfortunate pattern, Tim must first heal his hatred of God for creating women. He does not view God as female, but he still connects God to his bad experiences with women, which go back to his mother dying when he was an infant. He hates his mother for abandoning him (and thus all women), and he hates God for taking his mother away. When Tim heals his hatred of God, he will feel differently about women. Then he will attract women he likes. It will take a while for them to get to him because the old hatred is still out there collecting more angry women for him. As his old, "negative" thought-forms which are floating around in the airways dissipate, the new, healthier pattern will emerge, and he will attract women who like men.

The Outraged Home Buyer

Sal, a thin, desperate-looking man in his mid-forties, bought a home with a major water problem in the finished basement. He hoped I could solve his problems. I couldn't. The water problem was obvious: the carpets were mildewed, the baseboards were rotted out, and there were water stains on the walls. Sal said the seller and broker assured him the water problem was an old one and was no longer active. I said I thought he should have verified that claim by having the home independently inspected before he bought it. He said he did not do that because he trusted the seller and the broker. I told him I could not represent him—that I felt he was at fault for buying a home with obvious defects. He exploded, screamed that he would not allow himself to be run over, and stomped out of my office.

Curiously, he called from time to time to let me know how his case was progressing. He reported the seller and

the broker to the attorney general, the consumer protection agency, and the Better Business Bureau. They took
no action. Undaunted, he found an unscrupulous lawyer
who filed a lawsuit. The case dragged on for years and
was eventually lost. Sal continued to call from time to
time to rehash how he had been fleeced: the judge was
biased against him; the jury was wrongfully prejudiced
against him by the other lawyer; and his lawyer handled
the case poorly. He never learned anything from his case
because he was too angry and defensive to open his eyes.

So what was this case about for Sal? Take a moment
to unravel it on your own, before reading further.

What really jumps out for me is Sal's suicidal approach
to life. The danger signs about the wet basement were
everywhere, yet he believed what the seller and the broker
told him. Sal's inability to protect himself from obvious
danger tells me he suffered severe child abuse at the hands
of someone he dearly loved, almost certainly a parent.
He believed he could not object, otherwise the abuse
would have increased and what love he was getting would
have been withdrawn. He was in a deadly double-bind,
and came to view himself as a perpetual victim.

Sal probably went through life doing things to reinforce
the belief that he was a hopeless, helpless victim. He saw
Earth as a terrible place to live, and he blamed God for
everything. His rage towards God and the person who
abused him fueled his lawsuit which probably cost him
more than it would have cost to repair the water problem
and replace the baseboards and carpets. Lawyers call such
lawsuits, "mad money lawsuits." The client says, "I don't
care what it costs, I just want that S.O.B. to pay for what
he did!" Those are the words of someone very isolated
from God. As are these words: "I forgave them, but they
have to pay for what they did!" Where's the forgiveness?

Sal needs to separate God from the person who abused him. That will give him a different view of life. If he doesn't do that, he will continue to put out this message into the air-ways: "I'm a victim; come take advantage of me to prove I'm a victim!" And unscrupulous people will continue to come to him. Reconnecting with God will be difficult for Sal, for it will require facing the hatred he feels towards both God and the person he loves more than anyone in this world. He will need God's help to heal those wounds. The next case also involves the "Why me, God?!!" question.

The Medical Malpractice Victim

Eighty-year-old Anna came to me complaining of multiple aches and pains, arthritis, and poor range of motion. When I work with someone having physical symptoms, I almost always try to get them to look at the underlying causes, which are seldom physical. Anna harbored a great deal of bitterness and complained about many things. Her life had been a series of "Why me, God?!!" experiences. As a result, she had a love-hate relationship with God.

The primary focus of her physical complaints seemed to be in the area of her appendix. I asked what had happened to her appendix? Here's what she told me.

When she was nineteen, she developed what her doctors suspected was an abdominal infection. Exploratory surgery was scheduled, and the surgeon came into the operating room just off a week-long drinking binge. He opened her up, discovered an abscess beside her appendix, put his hand in, and burst it. The proper procedure would have been to put a suction device on the abscess and suck the infection out of her. The infection spread all over her abdominal cavity. She was sick for years, and had many surgeries to remove the infection. Her belly became a mass of scar tissue. People did not sue doctors for malpractice in those days, but the hospital did revoke this one's hospital privileges.

I asked how that had affected her life? She said, before the surgery, she was a beautiful, lively young woman, with many suitors in hot pursuit. Her life was one romantic adventure after another. Of course, there was no sex! After the operation, she felt as if her bubble had burst. She became shy around men. Two engagements came and went. She just did not feel safe letting those men see her scarred body.

I knew from the history Anna had given me that she eventually married a man whom she deeply loved and with whom she enjoyed a lengthy marriage until his death. So I asked what was so different about her husband that she could allow him to see her body? "Oh, he was 'Mr. Right!'" she exclaimed. I asked would she have met "Mr. Right" if she had not had the run-in with the surgeon? "No!" she exclaimed without thinking. Then she gave me a strange look and said, "You don't believe things work that way, do you?" I smiled and said, "God works in mysterious ways; this seems as good an explanation as any, doesn't it?" She just looked at me. "Perhaps that butcher of a surgeon did you a big favor, getting you off the social circuit so that 'Mr. Right' could find you?"

Anna did not want to take this view of what had happened. Even so, I could tell a deep part of her was in agreement because she left experiencing a significant improvement in her physical symptoms. The surgeon had interrupted what might have proven to be a life of endless parties and shallow relationships. Anna could have chosen to get off the social circuit herself, but she was having too much fun to do it. So she got nudged in a better direction. Her life improved even though she was not able to appreciate what had happened. It could have improved a lot more had she been able to release her resentment towards the surgeon whose bungling led her to her beloved husband. And it could have improved immeasurably had she been able to thank God, instead of blaming "Him," for sending the surgeon.

The next three cases involve a sensitive area. Please read the material before you slam this book shut and throw it away. Then let your soul advise you what is correct.

The Angry Feminist

Sally's father sexually abused her. She married the first man who came along, to get away from her father. Her husband had a series of affairs, each of which Sally discovered and "forgave." After many such affairs, she got fed up and sued for a divorce. She hated her husband for his repeated betrayals, herself for repeatedly forgiving him, and God for making men. She then went through a series of unsuccessful relationships with men, and three more divorces. She became a zealous feminist, taking up with women like herself who also hated men.

Abusive men were not her problem; they were only the symptom. Her problem was her hatred of men, God (whom she viewed as male), and herself. She rejected men and God, and usurped the masculine role. She believed she had to do that to protect herself. Unfortunately, in doing so, she made matters worse. She needs to separate God from men. She will find, I think, that God is not like the men she has encountered. As she feels safer with

God, she will feel better about men. Then she will attract men who like women. The next case continues this theme.

The Rape Victim

Janice, an attractive woman in her early fifties, returned from a vacation. I asked, did she have a good time?

"All except for one thing that happened," she said softly.

"What was that?"

"While out for an evening walk on the beach one night, I was assaulted and raped by two men. They left me lying on the beach otherwise unharmed, and ran away. I saw one of them left his shirt, so I called after them to come back for the shirt, which they did."

I was stunned. Janice looked me in the eye and said, "I knew I forgave them, right then and there; I haven't had any hard feelings since then; I wasn't damaged." Although she sounded sincere, something felt off to me. Many women who experience rape have a "denial" reaction. That is how they defend against the horrible feelings they have about what has happened to them. This is terribly destructive because they turn their rage inward—against themselves. They first need to experience and release their rage. Then they need to allow themselves to look at the big picture, so they can see what they need to do to heal.

So what was the big picture in Janice's case? I knew from earlier talks with her that she had had many difficult relationships with men, beginning with her overly critical father. Her first husband beat her, and her second one spent most of her money on bogus business ventures.

Then came a string of brief relationships with unreliable men who mooched off her without paying their fair share of the expenses. She ran each one off, each time swearing she was through with men, but before long she had another one living with her. She developed an intense hatred of men, of herself for allowing them to repeatedly take advantage of her, and of God whom she equated with her father when she was very young. Under the law of cause and effect, that hatred must come back to her until she heals it. As long as she confuses God with abusive men, hates men, and hates herself, she will attract men who hate women. And she may attract something else, too, if she is not careful. Consider the next case.

The Second Rape Victim

Sarah contracted breast cancer. Her doctor referred her to one of my teachers, Dr. John Upledger, mentioned in my opening remarks. John began to work with Sarah, and she went into a hypnotic trance. She spoke in a jiving, black male voice. (Sarah is Caucasian.) The voice identified itself as "Big C" and said, "We're the cancer, man!" Big C said Sarah had been raped in her late teens by an unknown assailant and again in her early twenties by a date. She became embittered, and said to herself, "What the hell, if I'm going to be raped, I might as well give it away!" So she became promiscuous.

Big C said, "We sent her endometriosis to warn her that she was hurting herself, but she did not listen. She went to a doctor who prescribed a drug which got rid of the endometriosis, so we had no choice but to send her another message—the cancer." John said he brought Sarah out of the trance and talked with her about what Big C had said. She got angry about being found out, then she cried. John worked with her around forgiving her assailants and herself, and she later underwent successful surgery. John told me he had never heard of the drug Big C said was used, so he later looked it up in the *Physician's Desk Reference* (PDR). "It had a name as long as your arm," John said, "and it was highly unlikely that Sarah could have consciously remembered it."

So why do you think a black male symbol was "chosen" to help Sarah? Please turn the book over and ponder this a moment before reading further.

Here's what I think happened. Men had become an evil blackness for Sarah. To heal that evil blackness, she had to experience men in a different way—one that was totally opposite from the way she normally viewed men. Spirit achieved this by taking on the form of a benevolent black man who told Sarah what she needed to know and do to cure her cancer.

Although I cannot know this for certain because I did not work with Sarah, my hunch is she had a life-long history of hating men, a male God, and herself. If so, the rapes were not isolated events; rather, they were the result of her hatred. This suggestion is not made to infuriate women; it is made to alert them to how they may unwittingly set themselves up for difficult experiences at the hands of men, whether by rape, other forms of violence, or psychological abuse. Certainly, men who abuse women need to be dealt with. However, I question whether focusing on punishing the man is the best initial approach because it has been my experience that women who do that are diverted from looking at themselves. I think the first order of business for women is to explore and correct their hatred of men, God, and themselves before correcting the man who acts as their mirror. And I think the reverse is true for men who hate women, God, and themselves.

———————————

The next four cases, which will round out this chapter, are ones in which people faced and began to heal their disconnection from God.

The Angry Widow

Dorothy came to me after her husband died of Lou Gehrig's disease, a slow, creeping paralysis which is ultimately fatal. She said, "I nursed Sam for three years, waiting on him hand and foot. We had a lovely marriage." Yet it was clear that she was enraged at Sam for dying, leaving her all alone, and at God for taking Sam from her. She drank too much and complained about her awful life to her friends, relatives, business associates and lawyer. Compounding her woes were legal problems: collecting the insurance for Sam's home care, and the embezzlement of funds by her supervisors at the shelter for the poor where she worked. "I raised a lot of that money those bastards are putting into their pockets!" she exclaimed. She was determined to take these matters to court.

It seemed she had good legal cases against the insurance company and her supervisors. I asked if she was dealing with a man or a woman at the insurance company? She said it was a man. Then we had the following conversation. As you read it, notice the number of *men* involved.

"How do you feel about this man at the insurance company?" I asked.

"I feel he and his company are stealing from me!"

"And your bosses. Are they also men?"

"Yes."

"And how do you feel about what your bosses have done?"

"The same way, like they stole from me and from a lot of other people, too!"

"And how do you feel about your husband?"

"What do you mean?" she asked, looking puzzled.

"Do you feel that *he* stole from you, too, by dying?"

"I sure do! I am mad as hell at him for leaving me!" she said, then put her hand to her mouth as if to take back what she had just said.

"Are you mad at God, too, for taking Sam from you" I asked. (She was Catholic, and so, for her, God was male.)

She nodded, as tears began to well up in her eyes.

"Are you also mad at yourself, for being mad at Sam and God?"

Dorothy looked at me and burst into tears. She cried deeply for several minutes. When she stopped crying, I asked if she was willing to do an imagination exercise? "Sure, why not?" she responded. I invited her to imagine Sam was standing before her. This she did quite easily. Then I suggested she ask him what, if anything, he had to say to her. She did this and began to cry deeply. Once she regained her composure, I asked her what had occurred? She said, "Sam asked me to let him go; he said he forgave me for being angry with him—that he loved me and would be waiting for me when it was time for me to leave."

She was open, and Spirit spoke to her in a way she could accept. I asked Dorothy to turn inward again and ask *her Sam* what she should do with her life. She did so and began to cry again. When she stopped, I asked what had happened. "He said for me to help families struck by fatal disease," she said. "I know what to do because I did it with him!"

When next I saw Dorothy, she said she had stopped drinking so much and had gotten a job at a local hospital working with families of dying people. She had put the insurance and welfare thefts behind her and had gone back to church. She enjoyed life. She had found her life's work. Her soul was in command.

Dorothy had more to do in her life than simply be a wife and mother. She may never have moved into the healing work, or reconnected with God, had her husband lived. It was a painful but necessary transition. The thefts by the *men* at the insurance company and the shelter were waking dreams reflecting what held her back: her rage towards her husband and towards God. Spirit came to Dorothy through male symbols because she needed to heal her relationship with both her deceased husband and her male God. Female symbols would not have worked for her.

Dorothy did not see all this, and it did not matter that she did see it. All that mattered was that she turn her attention toward what she needed to face. She did that, and her life got better. Had she focused on her legal problems—the clues—her life would have gotten worse. In all probability, sterner messages would have been sent to help her see the big picture. Or she would have drunk herself into oblivion.

Lawyers handle many "death" cases in which a spouse, sibling, or child has died. Dorothy's case is not how most such cases turn out, as any lawyer who handles will and probate work can tell you. More often, the surviving spouse, parent, child, or sibling never really recover from the death of a loved one. For instance, surviving spouses have relatively shortened life-spans. Surviving siblings and parents often experience severe and lasting emotional disturbances, and become physically ill. Instead of moving into the next phase of their lives, the survivors atrophy. This can be be partially or wholly avoided by dealing in a timely manner with the rage the survivors feel (usually unconsciously) toward the departed one, toward each other, toward God, and toward themselves.

The Man and the Beast

Charles came to me for help with his third divorce. One of his main interests in life, he said, was a passion for saving (rescuing) endangered animals from extinction. He spent so much time saving endangered animals, his marriages failed. As we worked together, he revealed a bizarre fact: he had suffered all of his life from an acute fear of being attacked and eaten by a supernatural beast. I asked if he was interested in learning what this beast was all about? "Sure!" he said. I cautioned him not to be too eager. "What do you mean?" he asked.

I explained such a thing usually represents that which we are not prepared to see in ourselves. He asked what I meant, and I said I did not want to put ideas into his head—that we should let the beast tell its story. Charles said he wished to proceed, and I asked him to close his eyes and allow the beast to come into his imagination—

that he should take his time and let it show itself to him. The following conversation transpired.

"I'm getting it," he said.

"What do you see."

"A lot of black hair."

"Do you see the face?"

"No, I can't seem to get the face."

"Keep trying."

"I am remembering something."

"What?"

"I am seeing my mother beating me up!"

"How old are you."

"Two years old," he said and began to sob.

At that point Charles emotionally re-lived the entire experience. After calming down, he said, "I saw her black hair everywhere. Then I saw her angry face glaring at me. It was the beast's face. Wow! That was something!" he exclaimed.

I asked about Charles' religious beliefs. He said he despised church, and was agnostic. I asked if his mother had been a religious person? "Very much so," he said, "and it was crucial to her for me to be religious, too." I asked if his unconscious fear of his mother might have something to do with his agnostic views or with his obsession for protecting endangered animals like himself. He looked as if a light bulb had been turned on in the darkness.

Charles' mother was guilty of physical and emotional child-abuse. This was at the root of the many difficult relationships Charles had experienced with women, a lifetime of being terrified of the imaginary beast, and being unsure whether or not there was a God. Fortunately, Charles had channeled his fear of the beast into something constructive—protecting endangered animals. Although he was a zealot about that, I thought it best not to pursue it further at the time. I felt Spirit would work with Charles in a way that would enable him to continue his work with the animals, but from a more centered place within himself. Instead, we worked around his divorce, and he was able to resolve it in a much more peaceful way than he would had he not healed the beast within him. Later he told me he was going to church.

More people than you might think suffer from the fear of such imaginary beasts, and their cases do not usually turn out as well as this one did. For instance, do you think beasts such as the one in Charles could be in part responsible for men raping and killing women and young girls, or husbands abusing their wives and daughters? Do you think beasts like this could explain why men and women are so often determined to "kill" each other in divorces? Could a beast like this explain the behavior of Adolph Hitler? Manuel Noriega? Charles Manson? Jim Jones?

The Sexually-Abused Woman

Rachel came to me with problems in her marriage. She wanted to file suit for a divorce and leave the state with her children, to protect (rescue) them from their abusive father. As we talked, she revealed she had never enjoyed sex and attributed that to her father having sex with her when she was five years old. I asked why she thought he did that?

"My mother," she said, "married my father because he was *her* mother's favorite, and she wanted to make her mother happy."

"Is there any way to undo what has been done?" I asked.

"No." she said tearfully.

"Will you ever get the love you want from your father?"

She burst into tears and collapsed into the fetal position. She stayed this way for several minutes, re-living the deep pain and loss of never having fully known her father's love. It was necessary for her to go through this, for as long as she held any hope of undoing what had happened, she would never heal. Knowing of a loss is seldom enough to foster healing. The loss usually has to be *felt* .

When Rachel quit crying, I asked her to close her eyes and allow that deep part in her, the part which had always been ready to help her, come forward. She waited quietly. After a few moments she said,

"I feel something happening."

"What do you feel?"

"Something very warm, very calming. It's coming from here," she said, indicating with her hand the lower middle part of her chest.

"What do you think it is?"

"I *know* what it is. It's *God!*" she said with tears streaming down her face.

I asked Rachel what kind of relationship she had had with God in her life? "Terrible," she said. That was quite understandable, given what she had experienced with her parents. After this session, she told her father how she felt about what had happened. She was then able to work on her divorce in a different way. She felt more peaceful towards her husband, and decided she no longer wanted to run away with her children and rescue them from him.

Many women in this country have suffered sexual child abuse. Often they are unaware of this: they repress the awful memory to protect themselves from knowingly living with someone who has sexually abused them. Other women remember the abuse, but never bring it up. Either way, these women feel deeply traumatized by what happened, and their relationship with God is usually severed, especially if they view God as being male. As a result, they have terrible relationships with men. And the reverse is true, too, as the next case demonstrates.

The Religious Man Who Feared God

Toby was deeply troubled by a recent event: he had gone to his church-owned health club and found fathers with their young daughters in the men's locker room. Repulsed, he asked the manager what was going on and was told a new policy had been enacted under which parents could take young children into either adult locker room. He wanted to reverse the club's policy, by writing the newspaper and filing a complaint with the parent organization of his church. In other words, he wanted to rescue the children from what he felt was inappropriate exposure to naked adults of the opposite sex.

I suspected Toby's strong reaction meant he had experienced sexual child abuse, and he admitted he had: his sister abused him often, and his mother, knowing of the abuse, did not intervene. I asked if he would be willing to use this incident from the health club as an opportunity to work with the child abuse, and he said he would do that.

I asked about his religious faith, and he said he had experienced a religious conversion when he was twelve. As he put it, "It saved my life." Yet, he was still very withdrawn, lived in the country alone, and had had only a few, brief relationships with women. He wanted to marry and have a family, but was afraid of women and felt the world was totally unsafe for children.

I felt his real difficulty was being connected with only the male side of God, and asked him if he would try an experiment to learn what he needed to heal. He agreed, and I told him I would say something to him, and for him to simply notice what he experienced when he heard it. He agreed, and I said, "Notice what you experience when you hear me say the word," and I paused for a moment, then said, "God."

He flinched, then began to shake. I asked what he was feeling.

"Fear....abandonment.....rage!" he grunted.

"With respect to your mother?"

"No, with respect to God!"

I asked how old was the part of him that felt that way towards God? "About two years old," he said in a young, sad voice. That was the age he had become disconnected from his Creator, and it was also the age of many of the young children in the locker room, who reminded him of that painful event. The locker-room incident was a waking dream for him, and that was why he was so intent on saving the children who reminded him of himself.

Toby was distressed to learn he had not fully reconnected with God. He asked how God could heal in the past, indicating he believed the past could not be healed. I said God was infinite—that time did not exist in infinity. He let out a huge sigh, and his body relaxed. We then talked about his getting married, having children, and showing his children a different world than he had known. He no longer felt the need to correct the policy at the health club. Instead, he simply resigned and got a refund of his money.

Toby represents a problem most people do not know exists: boys who are sexually abused by either their mother or sister(s). This, too, has a terrible effect: a disconnection from God which shows up in their relationships with women and with themselves.

Exercise

Take a moment to reflect on the cases in this chapter. What do you feel after having read these cases? Fear, anger, confusion, understanding? These are the varied responses my clients have to seeing the big picture, and these responses seem to go with the territory.

———————————

There are many layers of lessons in a legal problem, but the core lesson, always, is healing our relationship with God, within and without. That requires entering the terrifying shaky zone and facing the truth, an experience which strengthens us and prepares us to face the other lessons mirrored by our legal case. You will notice as you read this book that I do not talk about God with every client. It is not necessary to talk about God to achieve spiritual healing; it is sufficient to simply enter the shaky zone and experience the truth, for in experiencing the truth, we experience God.

Chapter Two

Introspective Law

There are many layers of lessons in a legal problem. I try to help my clients probe into and find as many layers as possible, for the more issues they discover and work through, the better their lives go afterwards. My friends and I call this introspective process "swami-ing" when we help another person heal, being "swamied" when someone (bless their hearts) helps us, and "swamicide" when we help ourselves (as I did in the case of my son's death). This swami business demands courage, curiosity, and a sense of adventure, for we never know what we will uncover when we go exploring in this way. Usually, it's what we have managed to avoid all our lives.

Introspection also requires a willingness to postpone the negotiating, posturing, and battling which normally accompany legal problems, for it is impossible to work internally while pointing the finger at someone else. As Jesus said, "Take the plank out of your own eye first, then you will see clearly enough to take the splinter out of your brother's eye." Clients having the courage to complete the introspection process end up with a much different attitude about their case: they first and foremost want to fix themselves, and thus stop *their* lessons from being presented again. Many of these "exceptional" clients

(I borrow the adjective, exceptional, from Dr. Siegel, who uses it to described his courageous clients) simply decide to drop their case and get on with their lives. Sometimes that is not possible, or even desirable. Exceptional clients who decide to stay in their case proceed with an entirely different goal: seeking what is fair, rather than revenge or permanent financial security.

Most people initially have stiff resistance to this inward-first approach to their legal woes, for their ego hates seeing its reflection. They cling to their resentment and desire for revenge. They insist on telling me how awful the other side is—what the other side did wrong. It's always the same: it's somebody else's fault. I do not listen to their arguments or blame-casting. Instead, I turn them back to themselves. I ask, "How does this problem mirror something in you?" Some people cannot make this shift. I certainly could not have made it when my daughter, Nelle, was injured in an automobile accident.

Nelle's "Accident"

When Nelle was five years old, she was run over by a car while crossing the street on her bicycle. Fortunately, the car was a Volkswagen Bug and was going slowly. Even so, Nelle's left leg was practically amputated above the ankle. I flagged down a passing car which took us to the hospital. All the way to the hospital, I asked myself "Why this? Why again?" as memories of my son's death flashed through my mind. An orthopedic surgeon was called in. He sewed her leg together and gave her a sedative.

The next day, I went to the YMCA to play handball and blow off steam. I set up to take a shot and felt what seemed to be someone step on the back of my right ankle.

I collapsed onto the floor and looked around. There was no one behind me. I stood up and could not walk on my right foot. The next morning, I was in that same orthopedic surgeon's office. The diagnosis was a ruptured Achilles' tendon. My injury was in almost the identical place as Nelle's, except on the opposite side. That was a rather curious coincidence. The doctor put me in a brace, and said Nelle would probably walk before I would, which proved accurate.

For months, Nelle and I went to this doctor together for check-ups. We competed to see who would walk first. I was her encouragement, and she was mine. We bonded during this time of shared injuries and doctor visits. That may never have occurred but for her accident because I had not allowed myself to get close to her, fearing she would die like her bother. Although I don't believe Nelle made a conscious choice to be injured, I believe her soul made the choice nevertheless, and that my soul made a similar choice which caused my injury. Nelle needed to know love from me, and I needed to know love from her. I needed to heal my vulnerability with children, my "Achilles heel." I did not recognize the gift at the time. Instead, I got a lawyer friend to sue the driver of the Volkswagen, and I got even angrier at God.

Nelle's injury triggered Dianne's and my unresolved feelings about our son's death. That was so disturbing, we separated several months after the accident, and later divorced. We were still mad at each other, and it was better for the family that Dianne and I part rather than pretend everything was alright between us. Nelle forced us to confront what we had suppressed. Such is the power of the soul, even in children—especially in children. Had someone tried to get me to view Nelle's accident as being the result of Dianne's and my inability to resolve our son's death, I would have hated them. I was not ready to see the truth that would make me free.

Now let's look at cases involving other people, beginning with people who, like me, were not prepared to see the truth in the "heat of battle."

The Feminist

Mildred called me after reading my ad in a local journal. The ad read:

LAW AND SPIRIT

Legal problems mirror your unlearned spiritual lessons, lessons presented before and missed, lessons to be presented later if not learned now. Sloan Bashinsky, former practicing attorney.

She was anxious to tell me about her case, but I said first we should talk about whether or not we would be able to work together. I said I would not help her "prosecute" her case; rather, I would help her probe into it and learn what it had to say about her, which would probably be something she did not want to see. "Your ego will hate it, but your soul will love it," I said.

Determined to tell me about her case, she said in a miffed tone, "My case is about sex discrimination; how do you feel about feminine issues?!!"

"It doesn't matter what the issues are; whatever they are, they mirror similar unresolved issues in you," I replied.

"Well, then, what do you think my issues might be?" she angrily asked.

"Based on what little you have said, I think your case

mirrors your hatred of men and your hatred of yourself as a woman. If we work together, that is what we are going to try to heal. I will not encourage you in your case, because you first need to come to peace with men and with yourself. You will never do that by waging war against men, which I imagine you have been doing most of your life. If you heal this, you may decide that your case isn't all that important and drop it. Or if it is still important, you will probably want to proceed in a much different way."

After a brief silence, she said, "I don't think you are the right lawyer for me," and we ended the conversation.

That was the last I heard from her, so I cannot report how her case turned out. Her ego was not prepared to turn her legal affairs over to her soul.

Other people get a little farther into the process before bailing out. For example, one of the people who critiqued the manuscript of this book was at the time she read it a defendant in a bitter lawsuit. She called to say how much I had helped her. I asked, how had she been helped? She said she had put herself in the plaintiff's shoes, and had seen the plaintiff was a very unhappy person—that the lawsuit was simply a manifestation of that unhappiness. Because of that insight, she "forgave" the plaintiff (but remained determined to win the case).

I asked whether she had discovered her lessons in the case? She became defensive and changed the subject. I think she feigned forgiveness to avoid facing herself. That is not forgiveness; it is *denial*. This theme I often find in my work is one of the main barriers to taking an inward-first approach to our legal woes. The next two cases shed more light on the forgiveness barrier.

The Sexually-Abused Woman

Joslin, a haggard-looking woman in her fifties on a New Age path, realized while meditating that she had been sexually abused by her father when she was three years old. Finally, she understood why she was a lesbian—and why she had always had trouble getting along with her parents. Instead of telling her parents what she had learned, she spent all her money on therapists, none of whom were able to help heal her terrible wound. She was broke and barely getting by when we met. I asked if she had talked to her parents about it.

"Talking to my parents about this after so many years would not be the loving thing to do; I must forgive them!" she exclaimed.

"How do you feel inside as the result of being so loving?" I asked.

"I am in agony," she groaned.

"I would think you would experience inner peace."

"So it would seem," she sighed, rolling her eyes.

I was not able to help. She was too afraid of her parents' reaction to be honest about what she had learned. I see this convoluted thinking a lot: people say they are loving when they are in denial. Although it would not serve Joslin to unleash an attack on her parents, it would help her a great deal to tell them what she had learned and how she felt about it. The fact is, she has always hated her parents for what happened (albeit unconsciously)— her father for what he did, and her mother for not protecting her from him. Now she consciously hates them, and is tormented about that. She uses all her energy to avoid the confrontation and to feign love. As long as she does that, she will have no energy to really love them.

The Nice Veterinarian

A similar case involved Roland, a veterinarian and devout Christian. A client came in with a puppy and asked Roland to trim its ears. The puppy had an infection and Roland advised the client to wait—that trimming the puppy's ears might endanger its life. The client insisted on the procedure, and Roland complied. The puppy developed a massive infection and died. The client hired a lawyer who wrote Roland a threatening letter. Roland was distraught, called the lawyer, explained what had occurred, and the lawyer decided not to take the case. Even so, it was a traumatic experience for Roland, one he could have avoided by standing his ground with his client.

Roland has had trouble saying "no" all of his life. This probably dates back to his childhood experiences with his parents, in which he found if he said "no," he would be emotionally rejected and abandoned, or even physically harmed. This case presented in waking-dream fashion an opportunity for him to begin healing in the present a life-time of saying "yes" when he meant "no." Being a good Christian, he gives people whatever they ask for. My hunch is, he often uses his faith to avoid his inability to say "no," and instead of taking him to heaven, his faith makes him miserable.

It is difficult to imagine how Joslin or Roland could be forgiving. Deep inside they surely hate themselves for not being honest. This self-directed hate must surface in some way, by moodiness, sniping remarks, substance abuse, or physical or emotional illness. This is the result of pretending to be forgiving and loving. The next case illustrates how awful false forgiveness can make matters, as well as the healing which can come from being authentic. This is the first introspective case I handled.

The Battered Home Seller

Jeri called me at my home in Birmingham (where I then lived) from another state after reading my book, *Selling Your Home, $weet Home*, which she had found in her town library. Her town was small, and the likelihood of it carrying my book was remote. That Jeri found me at all was curious, for I had just returned to Birmingham after living elsewhere for nearly three years. We were struck by the "coincidence."

She said she was involved in a terrible lawsuit as the result of selling her home, and she wanted me to advise her about it. "It's affecting my life so much, I have made an appointment to see a spiritual advisor!" she exclaimed. I said I found that to be interesting because I no longer practiced law, but I did offer spiritual counseling at times. While I had never done it with respect to a legal case, I was willing to try. She appreciated the additional coincidence, and agreed to work with me. Here is her story.

The day after the closing, the buyers instructed the closing attorney to stop payment on the $80,000 check he had written to Jeri. They claimed she had lied about the condition of the home. It later came to light the buyers were con artists who hoped to force her to settle for less money. Jeri hired a lawyer who promised to get her money back within a "couple of weeks" and to collect his fee from the buyers. This did not happen, and the case dragged on for months. The lawyer negotiated a tentative settlement for the buyers to pay $65,000 out of which he would take his fee. Jeri rejected the offer. Shortly afterwards, she met the buyers on the street, and they assaulted her, fractured her skull, and she was hospitalized.

Jeri interviewed another lawyer about suing the closing attorney and her first lawyer, adding an assault and battery claim, and continuing her lawsuit against the buyers. He declined to sue her first lawyer, but agreed to handle the other matters, and she hired him. He promptly negotiated a settlement with the buyers for payment of $80,000, out of which he would take his fee. "I can't believe all of this has happened to me; I never did anything to deserve this!" she cried.

I asked why she sold her home? She said she had owned it about twenty years, the first ten years she had lived alone, enjoying her life, friends, and work. Then she married. The marriage was good for two years, then a son was born. Her husband resented the boy and the loss of her attention. He cursed her, and she became depressed. Christian relatives came and converted her. They told her to forgive her husband, accept his abuse, and obey him, saying it was God's will she do that. She followed their advice and got even more depressed. Then, her husband began to complain about her home. He mounted a campaign for her to sell it. Further depressed, she caved in to his demands. Then came the legal nightmare above.

"My God, I set myself up for this, didn't I?!!" she gasped incredulously (the ego's instinctive response to such revelations). Then she laughed. I asked why she laughed, and she said, "I don't really know. Somehow this feels like a great big joke—on me!" Jeri had just committed swamicide, with a little prodding from me. I said it was good she could laugh under such circumstances—that

God often did "funny" things like this to get our attention. I then asked her to think about taking the settlement and dropping the other cases. "But they all need to be taught a lesson!" she exclaimed.

This was an ego response, one that needed to be honored to gain her ego's cooperation. So I said I agreed, but wondered if she helped them learn their lessons, would she play the *avenging victim* and be diverted from learning her own? I reminded her of how she had set herself up before, and we ended the conversation. She called several months later to say she had put "teaching people lessons" behind her and was dealing with the deeper issues—her relationships with her husband and her relatives, and with *herself*. I cautioned her about punishing her husband and her relatives for the way they had treated her, unless she wanted some more lessons. Afterwards she called to say she had worked though her problems with her husband and had distanced herself from her relatives.

Let's peer deeper into this case. Although Jeri had good reason to be mad at the crooks and her lawyers, at a deep level smoldered similar feelings towards herself for caving in to her husband and relatives. She misdirected this self-hate outward. Her initial "It's all their fault!" reaction was what psychotherapists call "denial" and "projection." Jesus called it, "throwing the first stone." The ego does this to avoid looking in the mirror. Had Jeri continued her legal fight, she would have learned nothing from her case. She would have only reinforced what I suspect had been a life-long habit of blaming others, chance, or God for her choices.

It was critical for Jeri to see the truth that would make her free—that she had co-created her difficulties. I led Jeri to the entrance to "the valley of the shadow of death," where she had to face the inner dragon, her inner Satan.

The dragon was not her husband, not her relatives, not the buyers, not the lawyers, not a satanic beast, and not God. It was herself. In facing herself, Jeri opened the window to healing.

Many people who previewed this book were uncomfortable with the outcome of this case. They raised several questions which I now answer. Perhaps in doing so I will also be able to answer any lingering questions you may also have.

Question 1: What about the buyers, the closing attorney, and Jeri's first lawyer? Do they need to be taught a lesson?

Answer: Yes. They will be given many chances to learn their lessons without Jeri's help. We cannot know how this will happen, but we can be sure that it will. They will be taught just loudly enough to get their attention— if they are listening. They will not be taught with vengeance, and neither should Jeri teach them that way. If she does, that will be reverse swamicide, more like suicide, for she will certainly invite a lesson about vengeance under the law of cause and effect.

Question 2: What about the money Jeri lost?

Answer: It is true she lost some money. Assume she had $3,000 in medical expenses and paid her second lawyer $10,000. That comes to a $13,000 out-of-pocket loss. But is it really a loss? What is the value of healing? Would you pay $13,000 for it? Would you pay everything you own for it? Many people have paid far more than $13,000 to therapists and teachers and have not healed. Jesus described healing as being the priceless pearl. Could it be Jeri got a bargain?

Question 3: What if the buyers had refused to pay

anything? What would you have advised Jeri to do?

Answer: Under this scenario, Jeri should proceed with her lawsuit—*after putting her own house in order.* If she prosecutes the lawsuit first, she will not learn her lessons.

(As a personal aside, Jeri's case answered my early questions and doubts about returning to the law and writing this book. I sensed she would be the first of many such people with whom I would work in this fashion. I had no idea how more people would find me, but I never doubted they would. And they did.)

Although the facts in Jeri's case are bizarre, it is a representative case. Here's why. All the people whom I counsel first want to cast all blame onto the other side. As we unravel their case together, most of them discover to their shock that they have done something in the past to set in motion events which later culminated in their legal case. Then they realize they are really enraged at themselves. Their ego hates seeing this, but their soul loves it because it is an opportunity for healing.

Not all my clients are able to go through this process: they are too defensive to take responsibility for having co-created their problems. The idea that their legal problems are the result of the law of cause and effect is something they simply cannot accept. They cannot embrace that concept any more than they can face their disconnection from God. In fact, the more they resist the suggestion that they have co-created their own legal woes—the more they seek revenge—the more disconnected from God they become. Conversely, the more they are able to take responsibility for what they have co-created, the more connected to God they become.

———————————

Another form of misdirected rage is seen in cases which trigger repressed emotions connected with having been previously abused, usually in childhood. The current problem consciously or unconsciously reminds them of the past abuse; the old, unresolved rage is aroused and dumped in the present, creating an over-reaction in most cases. The next case, the presentation of which is rather lengthy, demonstrates both forms of misdirected rage— towards self and towards people who were abusive in the past. It also demonstrates the curious and sometimes amusing dance my clients and I often go through as we work together.

The Enraged Man

John came to me after being arrested for driving under the influence of alcohol (D.U.I). He claimed he was innocent, and it seemed from what he told me he was. He said he worked a 4-12 a.m. shift at work. On the day he was arrested, he awoke at about 3:30 a.m., realized he was running late, and hurried off to work. A policeman pulled him over for speeding, listened to his story about being late for work, and asked him to take a breath test. John said he got mad, refused the breath test, and the policeman cursed him, ticketed him for speeding and D.U.I., and took him to jail.

I asked John why he refused the breath test if he was innocent? "I don't really know; it was a gut reaction," he said. I suggested his refusal to take the test had created a strong legal presumption he was guilty, a presumption that might be very hard to overcome in court. John's face flushed, and he said angrily, "I don't care, I will take this case to the U.S. Supreme Court, if I have to! Then, after I win, I will sue the police department for damages and get those cops fired!"

I suggested he might not win his D.U.I. case and, in any event, he would not easily find a lawyer who would file a damage suit against the police department. "Why?" he asked, defensively. "Because you acted guilty by refusing the breath test, " I replied. He glared at me, and his face turned crimson. I said I was not sure he and I could work together because it seemed he was more interested in getting revenge than exploring what his case might have to say to him. He glared at me again, then calmed down. I asked if he wished to proceed, and he nodded that he did.

I inquired about other brushes with the law that he might have had. He reluctantly admitted, shortly after the incident just described had occurred, he was arrested for urinating in public. The facts of this second case were as follows: he went for a walk in town late one Saturday evening, and stepped into an alley to tuck in his shirt because it was getting cold. A squad car drove into the alley at this moment, and the policeman driving it thought John was urinating in public and arrested him. He got into an argument with the officer—and ended up in jail again.

I pointed out that his anger in both cases caused things to take an immediate turn for the worse. He agreed, but argued the policemen had acted inappropriately. I reiterated he had made matters worse for himself by his reactions. Angered, he glared at me again. I renewed my offer to stop working, and he said, "No, I want to get to the bottom of this; let's go forward."

I asked whether there had been any other recent incidents in which he had become upset over someone else's inappropriate behavior? He thought for a moment, then slowly nodded. "Yeah," he muttered. "Shortly after the second arrest, I was riding my bicycle. I was in the left turn lane, and a passing pick-up truck swerved near me. I yelled at the driver, who backed up and swore violently at me. The guy was enraged, and I was afraid. I rode off in the opposite direction. He couldn't turn around, and I got away."

He looked puzzled, then appeared deep in thought. I asked if he saw the pattern of encountering *angry men*, overreacting, and things getting worse. He nodded. I then asked if he often got upset when other people behaved inappropriately? He said that he did—that he had been working on this with his therapist and his twelve-step group. The problem, he said, was associated with his father, who had mistreated him. "And the policemen and the driver of the truck acted like your father?" I asked. "Yes!" he shot back. His therapist and twelve-step group had encouraged him, he said, to seek vindication in his cases because they felt this would help him overcome what his father had done to him.

I asked if he could ever change what his father had done. "Well, he could apologize," John hedged. "And what if he doesn't?" I said, "Will you spend the rest of your life overreacting to what other people do and say, simply because you cannot let go of your anger towards your father?" John glared at me yet again, and I noticed I was no longer comfortable working with him. His ego was in charge, and I suggested we take a break so he could reflect on what we had explored. I offered to work with him at a later time, if he wished to work further with me, and we ended the meeting.

He called two weeks later to schedule another appointment. When we met, he sheepishly described a disturbing dream which occurred the night following our first meeting. In the dream, he was walking down a sidewalk minding his own business. A police officer accosted him and gave him a hard time. He yelled at the officer. The officer's face turned into the face of a horrible looking devil, and he pointed his pistol at John and pinned him on the ground. John awoke terrified. He realized the dream told him fighting back was not the solution—that fighting back only caused him more problems. Yet he still wanted revenge, but realized that, in trying to achieve it, he might end up the worse for wear.

This is the dilemma the ego always faces as it nears healing, and this is where I usually stop working with a client. This is the time of choosing between healing and misery, and only the client can make that choice. I have found, if I force a client at this point, then everything is undone. The ego takes over, and the healing opportunity is lost. I told John I had done all I could—that he would have to decide how to handle his cases.

He returned for another consultation after his cases had been tried. He said he wanted his lawyer to make the arresting officers look bad, but his lawyer advised against this because he felt attacking the police officers might cause the judge and jury to sympathize with the officers. "I was really angry at my lawyer," John said, "but felt I had no choice at that point in time but to follow his advice. He then won both cases."

Here's what John said happened. In the D.U.I./speeding case, his lawyer asked the arresting officer if he had smelled alcohol on John's breath or found alcoholic beverages in his car? The officer answered that he had not. John then testified about his odd job hours and waking up late, and the jury acquitted him on the D.U.I. charge and convicted him of speeding. In the second case, John's lawyer was able to get the arresting officer to admit he had not seen John urinating and had not seen urine or smelled urine. John then testified about being cold and tucking in his shirt, and the jury acquitted him in that case as well.

I asked John if he was aware his lawyer had used trial tactics which produced victory *without attacking the other side*? He looked confused. He saw what his counterattacks were doing to him, and even though he understood his terrible dream about counterattacking, he still was not convinced. So he was given another teacher—his lawyer. "Don't you see the hand of Spirit at work here?" I asked. He nodded, but it was clear he was not happy with the outcome.

I asked what would make him happy, and he replied, "I want those cops fired, and I want to be compensated!" I asked if that would heal his anger towards them, or towards his father? "Well, they deserve it, and I would feel better," he hedged.

"But will *you* be healed, John? How much money will you have to get to be healed? Will $5,000 heal you? $50,000? $50,000,000? Will any amount of money heal your anger, John?" I persisted.

"No, but I never did anything to those policemen to deserve being treated that way by them!"

We were going around in circles, so I tried a different tack by explaining that the anger he put out came back around to him. Like a magnet, it attracted angry people to him, and his over-reaction to their anger made matters even worse. I challenged him, saying he had co-authored his legal problems by hanging onto his anger towards his father (thus attracting similarly angry people to him), getting up late, driving too fast, not taking the breath test (thus acting as if he were guilty), and arguing with the policemen. While I appreciated his anger towards his father and the policemen, I questioned if his deepest and most important anger was the anger he *unconsciously* felt towards himself for having set up his legal difficulties?

His face sagged, and tears filled his eyes. He had seen the truth that would set him free—that he was really angry at himself and could not heal until he came to peace with himself. His ego surely felt as if it would die, for it could not deny that it, not the police officers, was responsible for what had occurred. I suggested he needed time to internally process what was coming up for him, and we ended the meeting.

I saw John one more time. He told me his therapist and twelve-step friends criticized him for not suing the police department and going after the police officers' jobs. I asked, did he wonder why they took that posture? "What do you mean?" he asked. I said I suspected that his therapist and twelve-step friends were also angry people whom he had attracted to himself, and my hunch was they wanted him to fight because that is what they had never been able to do for themselves.

"Damn, I believe you are right! They egged me on, and I would have taken all of the heat!" he said excitedly. I asked if that was how his father often treated him— egging him on to do what he did not have the courage to do himself? He gave me a knowing smile. I cautioned him about taking advice from others who encouraged him to focus outward before he got his own house in order. He said he would give serious thought to staying with his therapist and twelve-step group. Then he asked, "But what about those officers? They will do to others what they have done to me. Shouldn't something be done about them?"

This was one last effort by his ego to get revenge. I agreed with him that the officers had behaved inappropriately. However, I asked whether his attempt to correct them would embroil him in two protracted legal proceedings, which might draw him back into his old patterns? He thought about this, then said, "Probably, but something still needs to be done about them!"

I reminded him of the risks, and he said, "Yeah, this is pretty tricky isn't it?" (His ego was getting the message, albeit reluctantly.) I then asked him several pointed questions:

"Are you in the habit of pointing out to others their mistakes?"

"Did your father do that to you?"

"Did you like your father doing that?"

"Did you change when your father did it?"

"Do you think that the police officers will change if you go after them?"

"What is your real motive for going after them? It's revenge, isn't it?"

He squirmed in the chair. He wanted both freedom and revenge, and knew he could not have both. I suggested that the policemen would be sent other teachers to help them learn their lessons—that Spirit did not need his help here. A look of sudden comprehension appeared on his face, and he said, "I really don't have to worry about this being taken care of, do I?" He was then able to face the final and most important pieces—allowing Spirit to teach his therapist, his twelve-step friends, and most importantly, *his father.*

John courageously faced the truth about himself, and turned the teaching of others over to Spirit. In doing so, he went a long way towards healing a lifetime of attacking and counterattacking and telling others how to live, patterns rooted in his relationship with his father. He did it without going back into his childhood experiences with his father, a therapeutic method which had not worked for him. He did it in the only way that would work—in the present. His cases were vivid waking dreams in which most of his life lessons were embodied, and he did very well indeed.

Many of my clients are like John when they first come to me. With few exceptions, they have struggled with feeling victimized by their parents and other important people. They sincerely believe the way to heal these old wounds is to rehash them in therapy and transfer the family-of-origin fight into other areas of their lives—that fighting is the antidote for a life-time of running—that the cure for being passive is being aggressive. Unfortunately, it is not. Fighting in such cases only makes things worse because it reinforces the denial of having co-authored the problem. There are cases when fighting is appropriate, but this type of case is not one of them.

John's case had a big impact on a situation in my own life. I was embroiled in a running argument with a couple who had been good friends for several years. I was not comfortable with how they wrangled with each other over their new-born child, for their behavior reminded me of the events preceding my son's death. I told them of my discomfort, but I also did a good bit of extra preaching about it. They took this as an attack, and we went into the attack-counterattack cycle, each side proving the other side's faults. We got very angry with each other. I realized the parallel with John's case, and stopped telling my friends how to live. Although I was not comfortable being with them, it was not reasonable to expect them to change to suit me. I put the relationship on ice for an indefinite period of time, and relinquished the teaching role to Spirit. It was a liberating experience.

The Egotistical Homebuilder

Less dramatic cases are equally important. Early in my law practice, I represented Fred, a homebuilder. He was doing very well at the time he became my client, perhaps too well. He built homes on a speculation basis, meaning that he had no guaranteed buyers waiting to buy them when they were completed. Yet he sold every home before it was completed. He made a lot of money, but did not watch how he spent it or the ominous signs that the real estate market was due for a sharp reversal. He bought himself a Porsche, played golf a lot, went on fancy golf vacations to places like Hilton Head Island, Georgia and Bermuda, and took on many more jobs than an operation his size could reasonably handle in the time allowed by his construction lender. The better he did, the more egotistical he became, and the more he took on.

Sure enough, interest rates spiked as predicted and home sales went from a sizzling pace to practically no sales at all. Fred had twenty-five homes under construction. His construction loans amounted to $1,500,000, and the annual interest was more than $250,000. He was wiped out overnight and came to me for help. I told him I could play cute lawyer games with the construction lender and stall for a while. However, the lender would eventually sell the homes at a loss and ask him to pay the shortfall, since he was personally liable on the loans. His only option appeared to be a personal bankruptcy.

I suggested the names of two or three lawyers who specialized in bankruptcy law. Fred looked as if he would die. His face paled, and he leaned over and buried his face in his hands. He started to shake, then began to sob. It took him several minutes to collect himself enough to leave. I was afraid he might commit suicide. I did not know how to deal with such matters at the time, and was afraid to contact him to see how he was doing. It was months before I saw him again. I expected him to be angry at me for not following-up to see how he was doing. To my surprise, he was friendly and seemed quite happy. He gave me a big smile and shook my hand. I asked what had happened? Here is what I remember him saying.

"Well, I did sort of feel like killing myself—at least for a while," he said. "So I took some time off to think things over. I realized I had caused my own undoing— that I had been greedy, egotistical and careless in my business practices. I also realized that, although I am a damn good homebuilder, I am not much of a business-man. In fact, I do not even like that aspect of my line of work. I found some people with money and management experience and offered to build homes for them on a per-house fee basis, with them taking care of the money and management needs of the business. These people liked my proposal and put me back into business. Now I am doing what I like without all the hassle."

With respect to the construction lender, he said, "I went to the bank and told my loan officer he could have the houses back and make a bankruptcy claim for the de-ficiency. You should have seen his eyes bulge, as he realized he had right then and there become the proud owner of twenty-five half-built houses which he would have to finish. Of course, he didn't know the first thing about construction and had to hire a contractor to come in and finish the work. It was pretty funny. It's also funny seeing my fellow home builders hiring lawyers to fight off their construction lenders. It ain't worth all of that, just to lose in the end anyhow."

I strongly suspect Fred had been plagued all his life with feelings of never having been good enough—that no matter how well he did, it was never enough—a lack of intrinsic value. His egotistical, cavalier business practices reflected a deep wish to draw attention to his success, while blinding him to the otherwise obvious dangers. He finally achieved what he thought he always wanted, then his house-built-on-sand collapsed around him. Instead of playing the victim like his fellow home-builders, he looked around and saw what his situation told him about himself. That allowed him to design a job which truly suited him, and to deal with his creditors in a straightforward, honest manner. When it was over, his life was moving up, in sharp contrast to his fellow homebuilders.

Fred reminded me a lot of myself, and working with him was painful for me. My father and his father stressed grades, business acumen, and financial success, to the exclusion of the many other essential aspects of being. I never felt I measured up to their values, and developed a deep lack of self-worth. I compensated by being judgmental and arrogant. Had I been more awake, I could have learned much from Fred, and perhaps saved myself much time and grief. My ego feared the mirror at that time, and so I simply postponed learning the lesson a few years. Note: I did not fail the lesson; I simply postponed learning it.

Exercise

The purpose of this exercise is to allow you to ponder any lingering questions you may have about avenging yourself over a legal insult. Take a moment to think about people you know who have been involved in a legal wrangle and chose to fight. Do they still complain about their case? Are they still mad at their legal adversary? The other lawyer? The judge? The jury? Are they still responding to confict with altering submissive/avenging behavior? Did they learn anything from their case that helps them deal with conflict any better? If they won a large money award, did the money heal them? If not, how much money would have healed them? Would any amount of money have healed them?

Legal problems mirror important lessons for those willing to pause and probe into the deeper meaning of their case before proceeding against the other side. People who choose this inward-first approach to their legal woes experience healing and take a much different course of action than those who focus only on the legal symptom. In fact, focusing on the symptom simply postpones learning the lessons, for they will reappear in some other perhaps even more difficult context. These opposing results demonstrate the importance of turning the management of our legal affairs over to our soul and the teaching of others who do not ask for our help over to Spirit.

Chapter Three

Rescue Law

Today, many people are trying to cure themselves of co-dependence: needy, selfish, unloving behavior rooted in having grown up in an unloving, abusive, "dysfunctional" family. One of the most troublesome forms of co-dependent behavior is "rescuing." Most people have a rescue tendency, some more so than others. Those in whom it is strongest go through life trying to save victims-in-distress from their predicaments, and are miserable for it. Many crusading lawsuits are filed by rescuers to protect victims-in-distress, and many lawsuits are filed by victims against rescuers who fail in their rescue attempts. These curious phenomena, what causes them, and how to avoid them are the subjects of this chapter.

The Would-Be Ralph Nader

Jason called to discuss the recall notice he had received on his used Volkswagen. The notice appeared simple enough, requiring proof of payment for repairs for the defect covered in the notice and proof of ownership at the time the repairs were made. I asked had he submitted his claim? "No," he said. I asked why not, and he said, "I need time to prepare the case; I need the names of all people who made claims under this particular recall notice as well as those of all people who are entitled to make such claims."

I knew such information was known only to Volkswagen. It would have been unreasonable to require Volkswagen to furnish that information for such a small, uncontested claim. I was curious and asked why he needed that information? "I need it to prepare my case and to be able to alert all other owners of the affected Volkswagens that they should make a claim!" he exclaimed.

I thought Jason was somewhat over-zealous. I knew if he maintained his present course of action, his case would turn into a legal nightmare and would consume him. So I asked why he made it his life's mission to punish Volkswagen and to rescue all other owners of Volkswagens like his? "Someone has to protect the public, and I am going to do it!" he exclaimed. I asked if he was in the habit of fighting other people's battles? "The uninformed consumer has to be protected!" he retorted.

I was concerned about what might be underneath his desire to save the world from Volkswagen and asked whether he had done any co-dependence work? "Yes," he said, surprised. I probed further by asking if he knew about the rescue role? "Yes, I've worked with rescue stuff," he said, morosely. I asked if his approach to the Volkswagen recall was a rescue attempt? "Maybe," he said, his voice shaking.

I asked if he had friends who would be honest with him about this? "Such people exist," he said, weakly. So I suggested he talk to them about the rescue aspect of his case, file his individual claim, and get on with his life. He thanked me for my time, and we ended our conversation. I do not know how Jason resolved this case, for he never got back to me. I did not follow up with him because I seldom follow up with my clients. Rather I put all responsibility for doing further work on them. This keeps me out of the rescuer role, and teaches them to assume responsibility for their own healing.

There was an interesting personal aside to Jason's case I wish to share. About a week after he called, I experienced the revelations described in Chapter 2 about my daughter, Nelle, being run over by the *Volkswagen*. I believe the Volkswagen aspect of Jason's case triggered something in my unconscious mind that caused me to view Nelle's injury in a much different light. If so, Jason did me a huge favor by calling about his case. He also helped me look at the rescuer in me.

Many people think spiritual healing is all "hearts and flowers" or "love and light," which, unfortunately, is not true. People holding such sentimental views, adopted them to avoid the truth. And the truth is, people do unloving things to each other, and rescue behavior is one of the unfortunate results. It is important to know what creates rescue behavior, so we can stop creating it in our children. It is also important to know what rescue behavior looks like, so we can quit reinforcing it in ourselves and others.

People like Jason with strong rescue tendencies come from families where the family members, especially the parents, behave like victims. These parents have unsolvable problems, complain a lot, act helpless, and use guilt, shame, and seduction to lure their children into playing the rescuer role. The children repeatedly attempt to rescue or protect one or both parents (and other family members) from drinking, taking narcotics, being depressed, having job problems, and having a bad marriage. Often they protect one parent from the other parent, serve as a substitute spouse for one or both parents, and allow their parents to live vicariously through them. Children never succeed in these scenarios, but feel compelled to attempt the rescue in order to save themselves. If they do not, they risk being emotionally rejected and abandoned by their parents, or even physically harmed by them.

Another way in which such parents set up their children for playing the rescuer role is by repeatedly saying to them things such as: "If you love me, then you will/won't do _____!" and "I will love you if you will/won't do _____." The implied messages are, "I will reject and abandon you unless you do what I want you to do." The children do what is asked to save *themselves* and in doing so, lose themselves.

Children in such families feel compelled to play the rescuer role because they unconsciously equate rescuing with personal survival and not rescuing with personal destruction. The rescue never succeeds, and the children begin to feel victimized—that they can do nothing right, that life is hopeless, and that destruction is inevitable. They harbor enormous rage over living in hopeless terror of destruction by their parents. As they grow up, they transfer these attitudes and behaviors into their adult relationships. The myriad legal problems in our society are, in large part, expressions of this hopelessness, terror, and rage.

This grim picture is even more grave than I have painted it. At at the deepest human level, parents symbolically represent God to their children. The relationship children have with their parents is most likely the relationship they have with God, both within and without. Children who consciously or unconsciously feel victimized by, terrified of, and enraged towards their parents, fear and hate themselves and God, whether they know it or not. This is a serious charge, one I make only after having seen it proven many times. The last three cases reported in Chapter 1 were about people who became rescuers because of their separation from God. Please go back and review those cases from that perspective before reading further.

Emotionally-charged rescue activities are a misdirected expression of the rage the rescuers feel towards people who have abused them in the past—and towards God—and a symbolic (but futile) self-rescue attempt. Rescuers unconsciously believe that, by rescuing others in the present, they rescue themselves—that the more people they rescue, the safer they will be. I have found the more disconnected from God people are, the stronger their rescue tendencies are, and the more difficult it is for them to face the truth about their rescue tendencies, or how they came to have them.

The only way for rescuers like Jason to truly heal is to stop rescuing, which is very difficult for them to do because they are addicted to rescuing. Stopping their rescue activities is as difficult for them as going on the wagon is for an alcoholic or quitting heroin is for a heroin addict. For instance, if Jason had dropped his crusade and all other rescue activities, that would have triggered his deep-seated feelings of hopelessness, terror and rage. If he could have refrained from other diversionary or "fire-dowsing" activities which would have calmed the storm in him, those long-repressed feelings would have surfaced and washed through him, put him in the shaky zone, and caused him to feel like he was dying. If he could have stayed with the experience, he would have experienced significant healing.

This obviously is not a process many rescuers are willing to go through; they would rather take the heat off them-selves (and thus avoid the truth) by rescuing others. Such

71

people stir up legal controversy all over our country, and not in places where you might think to look. For instance, Tommy, a former lawyer, has devoted his life to working with people who are recovering from alcohol and narcotics, or who are children or spouses of such people. These people feel deeply victimized as a result of their childhood experiences. I shared these cases with Tommy.

He smiled and said, "Sloan, I have found many people who have been caught up in the peace and environmental movements are very much like your clients. They say things like, 'If only we could have world peace, then my personal problems would be solved,' or 'If only people would stop polluting our world, or killing dolphins, then everything would be okay.' These people usually have no interest in working on themselves. They crusade against some global problem to avoid doing that. Most feminists, gay-rightists, right-to-lifers, pro-choicers, and born-again people are that way, too. They use their causes to run away from themselves."

I later got that sinking feeling which usually precedes my committing swamicide, and called Tommy. I asked if he thought my book was a gigantic self-rescue attempt on my part. "What do you think?" he asked back. I saw him grinning through the receiver. I really did not want to know, a very good indication that the answer to my question was "Yes." After a few days, I recovered enough to face my ego motive for writing the book: to become a huge financial success to please my father, and even his father who had been dead for years, and thus rescue myself from what I perceived as their disapproval of me. I saw the trap and dismantled it. People would either buy the book, or they wouldn't. Unit sales were far less important than writing what I thought was true. That alone had to be my measure of success. That was all my soul required: being true to myself.

Before moving on, there is one thing I wish to clarify. Neither Tommy nor I think legal crusades are bad *per se*. Without them, many awful conditions would exist on earth. Tommy and I do not like environmental destruction, nuclear weapons, poverty, racism, sexism, abortions preventable by responsible birth control measures, or drunk driving. However we invite legal crusaders to ask themselves these questions:

"What is my true motive for participating in this cause? Is it to right a serious wrong, or is it to use this cause as an excuse to vent a life-time of unhappiness—to continue my fight with my parents and other people who have treated me badly?"

You have an internal barometer which can answer these questions. Simply notice how indignant and self-righteous you are about your cause. The more centered you feel, and the more compassionate you are towards your adversaries, as demonstrated by lawyers like Abraham Lincoln and Gandhi, or even Ralph Nader, the more likely your soul is directing a meritorious endeavor. The more indignant and self-righteous you feel, the more likely the hopeless, enraged, terrified child in you is directing a self-rescue mission. If your child is in charge, then your actions will come back to haunt you because you are coming from your hopelessness, terror, and rage, rather than from your heart. You get back what you put out: as you sow, you reap.

A different aspect of the victim-rescuer scenario is seen in malpractice suits. In the July 31, 1989 issue of *TIME*, the feature article entitled, "Doctors and Patients: Image vs. Reality," was encapsulated as follows:

"American physicians are teetering on their lofty pedestals. Never have doctors been able to do so much for their patients, and rarely have patients seemed so ungrateful. Today's doctors must contend with ever changing technology, ever threatening lawsuits, and a medical-industrial complex second-guessing their every decision. No wonder they often feel as sick as their patients."

I believe the American Bar Association would like to make a similar statement on behalf of lawyers. Being a lawyer is at least as tough as being a doctor. People feel victimized by life and contract an illness or experience a legal problem which confirms their unconscious belief that life is hopeless—that they are victims. Rather than take responsibility for how their attitudes, beliefs, and life styles have contributed to their problem, which would put them in the shaky zone and open the window to healing, their ego tells them to go to a doctor or to a lawyer who will hopefully perform a miracle and "fix" them.

It has been my experience that most people with medical, legal, or other problems do not really want solutions. They want miracles, and, failing that, they prefer to complain, blame someone else, and get revenge. When doctors and lawyers provide human solutions, instead of miracles, they hear, "Yes, but, that won't work because........!" "I already tried that!" "You don't understand!" and "If only so and so (or such and such) would change, everything would be all right!" These are ego statements. By defeating the rescuer, the ego confirms its victim belief that life is hopeless, reinforces its denial, and moves further into pain and misery, still hoping a Divine miracle will save it from itself.

The unaware rescuer is hurt, too. The victim's plight in some way resembles the rescuer's own plight. The rescuer has also felt victimized, and harbors deep hopelessness, terror, and rage. (That's why many doctors and lawyers choose their professions—to rescue as many people as possible, and thus themselves.) The unconscious motivation of the rescuer is *self-rescue*, and when the rescue fails, the rescuer feels tricked, hurt, and angry: an ego response. The rescuer retaliates verbally (or by sulking), which reinforces the victim's position and gives the victim justification for punishing the rescuer even more. The rescuer gets angrier (or sulks even more), and the situation continues to escalate. This ego-directed escalating spiral of rage is at the root of many medical and legal malpractice cases, as well as most domestic violence and child abuse.

Doctors and lawyers who attempt to rescue victim-in-distress patients and clients from their own creations, always run some risk of being sued for malpractice. Of course, the risks dramatically increase when doctors and lawyers do bad things, such as: make patients and clients wait past the time of their appointment; talk down to them; not listen to or spend enough time with them; or make their problems worse. That is what most patients and clients have experienced throughout life, and doctors and lawyers usually have the financial resources and malpractice insurance coverage to compensate them for the past and present insults.

I know I am in the rescuer-victim loop with clients when I catch myself either pressing them to take my advice or being angry at them for not taking it. When I am asleep, I proceed with the rescue attempt, and we get into the escalating victim-rescuer spiral. When I am awake, I decline the rescue and invite my clients to suggest solutions and make all decisions. This is a disturbing experience if they have spent most of their lives avoiding responsibility. But it keeps us out of the spiral, and often leads to healing. Rescue never leads to healing; nor does attack.

For instance, had I criticized any of my clients in the cases reported in this or the preceding chapters for not taking my advice, their egos would have taken that as an attack and would have jousted with me. If these people had been persuaded (a form of rescue by the lawyer) to prosecute their legal cases, that would have reinforced their old ego behavioral patterns and prevented them from healing. Jeri's lawyer (see preceding chapter), in particular, might have regretted encouraging her to prosecute her case rather than to settle it. Jeri was already unhappy with him because he would not sue her first lawyer and because he had recommended she take the crooks' $80,000 offer. Her discontent with him most likely would have increased because he could never have given her what she wanted—complete revenge. She already wanted to sue two lawyers, and he could well have become the third on her list!

Doctors, lawyers, and other professionals who sincerely want to do something about the threat of malpractice, will acknowledge their ego-centered rescue tendencies, which can only hook into their patients' or clients' own ego needs. A failed rescue is an invitation to ego retaliation, and cross-retaliation, and ultimately to being sued. The solution to the no-win rescue scenario is to invite clients to use their problems as opportunities for healing.

This invitation is directed to the soul. If a soul connection is made, then the likelihood of a malpractice suit is slim. Patients and clients seldom sue doctors and lawyers they love, even if they do not perform miracles.

Dr. Bernie Siegel establishes a soul connection with most of his patients, and I urge doctors, lawyers, and other professionals, as well as their patients and clients, to read Dr. Siegel's books, *Love, Medicine and Miracles* and *Peace, Love and Healing.* Adoption of his doctor-patient practices by doctors, lawyers, and other professionals will foster soul connections with their patients and clients, eliminate most malpractice lawsuits, and bring healing to all concerned.

I learned the hard way about the ego connection after the publication of my first two books, *Home Buyers: Lambs to the Slaughter?* and *Selling Your Home, $weet Home.* Those books assaulted the residential real estate industry, especially its practices which create confusion about whom the real estate agent really represents. I encouraged an "It's you against your Realtor" ego attitude and encouraged home buyers and sellers to continue, through their Realtor, their childhood fight with parents and other authority figures. Consumer advocates and home buyers and sellers loved those books. Most Realtors, on the other hand, hated them. Instead of bringing real estate consumers and Realtors together, I drove them farther apart. I did this because I was in a fighting mood at that time in my life. I had not worked through my childhood resentment or my own rescue tendencies, a fact clearly reflected in my writing style.

I recently talked with a Realtor who had read those books. He said the same thing about them I just said—that I had fostered even more animosity between buyers, sellers, and Realtors. He specialized in residential real estate and was terrified of being sued by his clients. His lawyer had drawn beautiful listing agreements, disclaimer statements, and waivers of liability to protect him from disgruntled clients. I said his lawyer's work might win lawsuits, but it would not *prevent* lawsuits from being filed against him by angry clients.

Realtors, especially those in residential real estate, are very much engaged in rescuing: helping people solve their home buying and selling problems. A person's home is, among other things, a highly-charged ego symbol. It represents survival, family, comfort, status, prestige, etc. It also reminds people of their childhood experiences at home. For people who had a bad home environment growing up, those unpleasant memories are brought to the surface when they buy or sell a home. Underneath those memories is their deep hope that they will someday find the safe, happy home they never had.

The advertising Realtors use—that they are friendly, trustworthy, reliable, helpful, protective, etc.—is aimed directly at these highly-charged ego needs. This is a set-up for a lawsuit. When something goes wrong, wounded buyers and sellers feel tricked once again, and dump a lifetime of pain, misery, and resentment on their Realtor. That reaction is aggravated when Realtors respond to client complaints with ego statements such as: "I'm not a lawyer—you should have hired a lawyer (even though I said you wouldn't need one);" "I can't remember saying that;" "You signed a disclaimer and a waiver;" or "I really represented the other side."

When home buyers and sellers hear these things—and believe me, they hear them often—they become enraged, for that double-talk reminds them of what they heard growing up. This scenario, seen all too frequently in residential real estate transactions, is unwittingly set up by Realtors making ego connections with their clients. If Realtors like my friend would relate to their clients soul-to-soul, instead of in an ego-centered "Let me help you, but don't blame me if things go wrong" way, their lives would be a lot easier.

How can they do this? For one thing, Realtors might be more honest. Instead of taking a listing at a price the seller insists on getting, Realtors could decline the listing when the seller wants too much. Instead of making promises about the quality of construction, zoning, the school district, or the state of the title (promises most Realtors are not willing to back up with their pocket-books), they could tell the buyer to investigate those matters. Instead of recommending the mortgage banker who has done the most for them lately, Realtors could shop around and find the buyer the best loan rate. Instead of pretending to represent the buyer, Realtors could be very clear that they do not (in traditional transactions) represent the buyer—that they have a duty to tell the seller anything of value the buyer discloses. Realtors, who claim to represent and expect to be paid by the seller, could stop saying to the buyer, "I shouldn't tell you this about the seller, but _____!" Instead of pushing clients to sign on the dotted line, Realtors could empower them by letting them make up their own minds. Instead of protecting themselves with lawyer-written disclaimers and waivers, Realtors could rely on their honesty and integrity to protect themselves.

There is one other thing Realtors could do: eliminate the charade about representing the seller. The fact is, Realtors represent *the deal and themselves*. Everyone knows this, so why pretend otherwise? Why don't Realtors just say they are match-makers? That would eliminate the confusion about Realtors' loyalties, the covert double-dealing, the surprises, and most of the lawsuits.

Most buyers, sellers, and Realtors would, I think, have a difficult time with this way of doing business. Here's why. As stated above, buyers and sellers are looking for the safe, happy home they never had, and Realtors have strong rescue needs which dove-tail into their clients' needs to be protected (parented). Realtors also have a strong ego need to be viewed as professionals, and not as middlemen or matchmakers—their primary function. My proposal challenges that paradigm. There would be no parents out there for buyers and sellers who would have to take care of themselves. Realtors would quit rescuing buyers and sellers (and thus themselves). Realtors would be service providers, not elite professionals. (And so what?) That change would send tremors throughout America because the victim-rescuer loop, in which the residential real estate market now operates, would be disrupted.

A similar paradigm shift could be made by doctors, lawyers, patients and clients. Instead of expecting doctors and lawyers to be the parents (or gods) they never had, patients and clients could use doctors and lawyers as service providers who may or may not solve problems the doctors and lawyers did not create. Instead of trying to rescue everyone in sight (and thus themselves), doctors and lawyers could simply provide services on a take-it-or-leave-it basis. Instead of claiming to be miracle-workers, doctors and lawyers could be ordinary human beings. Instead of telling patients and clients what they want to hear, doctors and lawyers could tell the truth. That would get rid of patients and clients who want miracles and sue when they do not happen. That system jump would cause so many ten-point-Richter-scale emotional earthquakes, we would have to declare a national healing holiday to give everyone time to go through the shaky zone together. How many people do you know who are not presently using a doctor or a lawyer?

Exercise

Take time to reflect on the material in this chapter. Is there anything here which reminds you of your own behavior or that of others dear to you? Of legal cases in which you have been or are presently involved? If so, what is it like for you to see this? What are you going to do about your new insights? If you are a lawyer, do you now have a different perspective of your client's cases and why you chose to be a lawyer? Of how you could be relating to your clients in a new way? If so, what are you going to do differently?

Underneath all lawsuits are unconscious motives. Resentment, the desire for revenge, and avoidance of personal responsibility are always there. Often present is our deep-seated need to rescue those whose plight symbolically resembles our own. Just as often, the motive is to get even with someone who has tried to rescue us, and failed. They failed because we would not let them succeed.

Chapter Four

Family Law

The previous chapters introduced the big picture and introspective approaches to legal problems, as well as the ego behavior fueling many legal cases. This chapter continues by giving special emphasis to cases involving families. Sayings such as, "The sins of the fathers are visited on the sons," "He's a chip off the old block," "She's a spitting image of her mother," and "As you sow, you reap," come in handy in these cases. It is important to understand what happens in our families because the children we birth and raise grow up and perpetuate the legal problems in our country. Let's look at cases which shed more light on this difficult subject.

The Enraged Step-Father

Polly made an appointment for her and her husband, Henry. She said he was having rage attacks and was taking his rage out on her and their children. I said I would see them together, but she should come prepared to look at her own rage as well. "What do you mean?" she asked. I said spouses are usually pretty good mirrors of each other—what troubles one usually troubles the

other. She said, "Well, I'm not mad about anything—
it's Henry who has the problem, and if he doesn't correct
it, I will leave him." I re-stated my caution, but could
tell it fell on deaf ears.

Polly and Henry came in. Henry was pleasant, and
Polly was rather moody. She interrupted him almost every
time he spoke. He politely indulged her. It took a long
time to get the facts out because of Polly's interruptions.
Here is what unfolded.

Henry hated his job, running the family business he
had bought from his father. Polly was the bookkeeper
for the company, and hated her job, too. Henry always
wanted to be a journalist, but his father ridiculed him
for that. Actually, Henry might have made a very good
journalist: when he was in high school, he won an
international journalism competition. Instead of doing
what he loved, he chose work he hated. I asked if he
still wanted to be a journalist, and a big smile appeared
on his face. Polly scowled and said, "You could never
make enough money doing that to support our family."
Henry's face sagged.

I suggested they needed to think about their work—
that as long as they hated their work, they would hate
themselves. I suspected much of Henry's rage was fueled
by his job dissatisfaction, and Polly was unhappy with
her own job situation, and was venting that unhappiness
by picking at Henry, rather than changing herself.

I thought something else was bugging her. Later, I
learned quite by chance from a mutual acquaintance that
Polly was having an affair. Seeing another man was most
likely a compensation for working with Henry at a job
she hated. Henry did not know about the affair, at least
not consciously. Unconsciously, he knew about it, and
that, too, was fueling his rage. Instead of facing herself,

Polly blamed Henry for everything. As a result, she and her children were the targets of his *overt* rage, and her *covert* rage.

There was a lot going on in this case, as there usually is in such situations. Rage is never the "real" problem. Rather, it is a symptom. In this case, there were two problems: infidelity and not doing rewarding work. These two factors, layered one on top the other, are often found in unhappy families. It is not always the wife who is unfaithful, or the husband who has the rage attacks. Just as often the symptoms are reversed. It doesn't matter. The result is the same. The family is destroyed because the parents are afraid to live their dream, or to allow each other to do that.

The hardest job in the world is being someone other than yourself. Being someone else destroys people and their families. There are other forms of dishonesty which destroy families, as the next case demonstrates.

The Bewildered Woman

Joan, an old friend who knew of my training in healing, came to me for help with problems she was having in a divorce. For years she was unhappy in the marriage and complained about it to whomever would listen. I advised her to get a divorce, or at least quit complaining to me. Instead of getting the divorce, she had two children to fill the loneliness and to "save" the marriage. The marriage got worse, and the children suffered deep emotional problems. Finally, Joan told her husband to move out, which he promptly did. Then her problems really began.

"I expected to feel free and happy," she told me. "Instead,

I came unglued. I am angry and terrified, which seriously affects my ability to function. I am bewildered about what is happening to me. My psychologist hasn't helped me. I have to regain my stability, or I will be unable to function! Can you help me?"

She was near the shaky zone, but was looking outward for healing. She needed to be nudged to look inward, so I said, "That depends."

"Depends on what?" she asked.

"On how much you are willing to look at yourself."

"What do you mean?" she asked, suspiciously.

"You have avoided dealing with this relationship for years. Now you are out of rope. If you really want to heal this thing, you will have to stop blaming your husband and look at what it is in *you* that is causing you to be so unhappy."

"Oh," she said quietly.

I did not speak, and after a few moments she said she was willing to give it a try.

There were three principal areas in which we worked. The first was the unexplainable emotional upheaval. Inasmuch as this case involved her relationship with a man, we explored her relationship with her father. She revealed that during most of her younger years her father had kept a mistress. "Mom and I knew about it and grieved that Dad was never completely there for us," she said. "Then, when I was fifteen, Dad suddenly moved out and went to live in another city with his girlfriend. There was never any talk or time to prepare. It was as if the door, which was never fully open, was slammed in my face!"

Joan experienced a deep, unresolved sense of abandonment by her father and the terror and rage which normally accompany being physically and emotionally abandoned by a parent. When he left, she consciously or unconsciously feared any expression of her violent feelings would close the door even tighter. So she repressed these feelings, perhaps knowingly, probably unknowingly. These feelings were still in her after all of those years, and her husband's moving out triggered them.

This was an opportunity for her to heal the wound around her father by telling him what his leaving had been like for her. This would have released what she had been containing—her rage and grief, which blocked her real love for her father and fueled her emotional upheaval around the divorce. Then she could approach the divorce without being affected by the past. She could not bring herself to talk to her father. Instead, she waged a bitter fight against her husband in the divorce. Much of the fight was, no doubt, fueled by the unresolved rage she felt towards her father and towards herself for her own poor choices.

Later, Joan came back and we worked on the second issue: her relationship to the truth. For years, she did not love her husband. Then she talked him into having children by pretending she wanted to be a mother, when her real reasons were much different. She complained to others about her husband, when she should have been observing herself. Her denial would not let her look inward.

I felt sure this denial was rooted in what Joan had experienced with her father. She was deeply hurt by her father's behavior but never felt safe telling him how she felt. This began a pattern of dishonesty with men who were important to her. Furthermore, she was so badly hurt by her father that she made an unconscious decision never to allow a man into her heart again. Although she "fell in love" with her husband and married him, her deep fear of being hurt again caused her to unconsciously do things to sabotage the marriage, and protect herself from more hurt.

As we talked about this, she began to squirm. It was not easy for her to own the choices she had made. Yet she could not deny she alone had made them. This freed her from her denial. A window opened for healing, and she began to come to terms with herself, to feel kinder about her ex-husband and his relationship with their children. Later she was able to enter into more healthy relationships with men. It was not an easy process for her, but as she said much later, "I am glad I went through it."

Note that throughout our work together, we focused on her side of the matter. No doubt her former husband had many lessons to learn in this case, but focusing on that would have diverted her from learning her lessons. She needed to learn her lessons so she could live a better life, instead of repeating the same no-win patterns with men.

The third issue involved Joan's children. She said, "I realize I do not really like being a mother full time, and now it seems I am going to be a *single* mother full time!" I asked her about letting her husband have more time with the children, which would give her more time to herself. She initially balked at this. Although she wanted more time to herself, she was more interested in punishing her husband by restricting his visitation than in allowing him to help her with the children. Eventually, she saw the self-destructive situation she was making for herself and extricated herself from it by agreeing to allow her children to spend more time with their father.

Joan is moving in the right direction. The belief that she is a victim is deeply imbedded in her. Ultimately, she will have to forgive herself for having created these difficulties. She will not be able to do this because I think its a good idea, or even because she thinks it is a good idea. She will only be able to do that by reconnecting with God, from whom she divorced herself because of her experiences with her father. When she does that, she will experience forgiveness because, in God's eyes, there is nothing to forgive. God loves us regardless.

There is another aspect of this case which deserves mention. It is an aspect I struggle with in my life, with respect to my parents and also with respect to my own children, and it is one I believe most people struggle with. There are many reasons people have children. All too often the reasons are to satisfy selfish personal needs not related to the needs of their children. Parents do this in a variety of ways. Having children to fill loneliness and to save a troubled marriage are ones we often see. Two other common ones are to have someone around on whom the parents can physically and emotionally vent their unhappiness, and to have someone around who will achieve what the parents could not achieve themselves.

I recall a time when my wife, Betty, and I talked with a wise friend about different matters of concern to us. Betty shared with our friend "how challenging my son, Evan, can be at times." Our friend smiled and said with a twinkle in his eye, "Evan's not *your* son, Betty, he's *God's* son; are you treating him like God's son?" That created a pregnant pause in the conversation, and caused both Betty and me to think even more about the true responsibility of parents.

A graphic example of parents who did not understand whose child they were raising occurred in the movie, *Dead*

Poets Society. The father expected his son to be what he (the father) had wanted to be—a doctor. The son wanted more than anything to be an actor. The father squelched his son's dream, and the mother stood by and watched. The son killed himself. Then the father launched a vendetta against his son's poetry teacher who had encouraged the boy to live his dream. Again, the mother stood by and did nothing. It's hard to know who the son hated most: his father for denying him his life, his mother for not intervening, God for giving him such parents, or himself for not being able to stand up to his father. I put my money on the latter.

I hope people who blame their parents for their lives not working will ponder *Dead Poets Society*. What is their deepest rage? Is it not the rage they harbor towards themselves for not living their dream? Does repeatedly rehashing in therapy or support groups the rage they feel towards their parents reconcile the rage they feel towards themselves? Will anything short of chasing their dream heal that inward-directed rage? Instead of chasing their dream and letting the dead bury the dead, most unhappy people focus on the past, run from their dream, and covertly commit the most horrible suicide imaginable. I know; I did that. And I know many other people who did it, too.

They hate themselves. They feel valueless, and seek value everywhere but in themselves. They engage in behavior which attracts attention: hysteria, over-achievement; illness; weird dress; dangerous driving; going up in a tower with a sniper rifle and shooting people. They run with bad people who stroke their needy egos. They chase lotteries, gamble, speculate in commodities and stock indexes, file money-damage lawsuits, steal, and sell drugs to make large sums of money, fast. Sometimes they feel so devalued they give up, as did the son in *Dead Poets Society*—as did the son in the next case.

The Heroin Addict

The Allgoods were referred to me to help their son, Jamie, a heroin addict and street thief. Before meeting Jamie, I had several meetings with his parents. They were angry at Jamie and mortified over how he was disgracing the family and his Christian upbringing. "Why, we gave him everything anyone could want, and look what he is doing to us!" they exclaimed.

The Allgoods both admitted drinking frequently, yet were critical of Jamie when he first drank, and again later when he experimented with marijuana. I asked if they thought Jamie might simply be acting as a mirror for their dependency on alcohol? They were closed to this idea, so I asked what would be the worst thing Jamie might say about how they had treated him as a child? Both agreed, "Jamie would say we never accepted him for who he was. He always had different interests from us."

I asked did they think his behavior might be a reaction to how they treated him? They looked pensive, but nothing further came of it. I was unable to get them to admit they had anything to do with Jamie's problems. The truth was too threatening to them. So I worked with Jamie alone. This reduced the odds of a successful outcome because much of his difficulty was rooted in his relationship with his parents.

When I met Jamie, I asked what had it been like for him in his family? "I was always the black sheep in my family," he said angrily. I then asked what one word best described how he felt inside? He thought for a few moments and said with a sad, faraway look in his eyes, "Rejected, I have felt rejected all of my life!" I asked if he thought there was any connection between his feeling rejected and his use of heroin? He looked surprised, but said nothing.

"What do you suppose would have happened to you if you had not turned to drugs?" I asked.

"I would have died, I suppose......"

"So the drugs had been a mighty good friend, to save your life, huh?"

He gave me a startled look, then said, "No one has ever said anything like that to me!"

I smiled and asked him to pretend that nothing bad would be done to him and, knowing that, what would be the worst thing he could do to repay his parents for rejecting him. He thought for a moment, then got this most amazed expression on his face. "Why, become a junkie, but that's crazy; I'm only hurting myself by doing that!" At that moment, he saw the lose-lose scenario he created for himself by participating in his parents' "scapegoat" strategy.

After gaining this insight, Jamie found he was more willing to let go of his habit. He was still mad as hell at his parents, but he did not want to kill himself as part of his revenge. Instead, he took a job doing work he always wanted to do, but which his status-seeking parents always opposed. Unfortunately, his assertion of independence so disturbed his parents, who still clung to their hopes that he would go to college and become a professional, that they mounted a campaign to bring him back into the fold. That was exactly the opposite of what he needed at this delicate time in his life. As a result, his unresolved childhood emotional needs for their love and approval overwhelmed him, and he relapsed. Returning to heroin and stealing was his way of escaping from his parents' rejection, and punishing them for it.

Jamie's is a sad story. Unfortunately, I often encounter similar stories in my work with adults who grew up in alcoholic, drug-addicted, or otherwise dysfunctional families. I have friends who have been in prison, addicted to drugs and alcohol, and who have worked within the criminal justice system. Without exception, they said they never met an alcoholic, drug addict, or prison inmate who was not severely abused as a child. I asked them if, by abuse, they meant physical or sexual abuse? They said physical and sexual abuse are often involved, but the deeper, more hurtful abuse is psychological battering.

The Bull-Dozed Heiress

Axel, a woman of high standing, called me long distance after having found and listened to an audio tape of *Kill All the Lawyers?*. She said she was embroiled in a horrible legal battle involving a chalet she had purchased in a ski resort, and wanted me to advise her about it. I asked her to tell me about her case.

She said she and her husband, Philip, had paid $150,000 for a chalet in upstate New York to use as a retreat. The contract provided for the construction to meet code requirements. They hired the city building inspector to inspect the chalet before the closing, and he said everything was as it should be. After the closing, they discovered many things were wrong with the chalet, including major leaks in the roof and through the foundation. They engaged an architect to inspect the property, and he reported

93

multiple code violations which would cost at least $80,000 to correct.

Axel said she called the builder and complained. He promptly sent a bulldozer over, and the operator bulldozed all the trees on the property, claiming, "The roots were causing the foundation leaks." Then he piled huge, ugly mounds of dirt up against the foundation, "To keep water away from the foundation." Again, she called the builder to complain, and he laughed at her. So they hired a lawyer in a nearby town to handle the matter. The lawyer they really wanted to use was the builder's lawyer. Their lawyer reached a settlement for them to deed the chalet back to the builder in return for the builder paying them back their money in two years. The only security for payment was to be the chalet!

This was certainly a bizarre case. I felt Axel and Philip needed traditional legal help here, otherwise they would lose a great deal of money. So I suggested they ask the New York consumer protection agency to help them, as it appeared they would need more firepower than they would ever find in a small resort town where everyone was best friends. Then I said I was curious why this might have happened, and wondered if Axel would be interested in trying to learn if there was some deeper reason for it? "Sure," she said, so I asked her to tell me how she came to buy the chalet.

She said several years earlier, Philip had been in Canada on business. He was to fly to New York City, but his flight was cancelled. Rather than wait on the next flight, he rented an automobile and drove into New York. He passed through the ski resort and really liked it. He always wanted to return. Their daughter, Melissa, had been dismissed from the university (and several others, previously), and there were no other suitable near-by colleges for her to attend. So they decided to enroll her in a New England school. There was one near the ski resort that appealed to her, so they traveled there to see it. While there, they decided to buy the chalet for Melissa to live in, thinking they would use it as a retreat when they came to visit her.

My curiosity about Melissa was aroused, and I asked Axel to tell me more about her.

"What does Melissa have to do with this?" She asked.

"I don't know yet, but somehow I think she has a lot to do with it," I replied.

"So, what do you want to know about Melissa?"

"Everything that happened with her after you bought the chalet," I said.

Axel said Melissa threw wild parties *in the chalet*, so she made Melissa take an apartment in the neighboring village in which the college was located. Then Axel learned that Melissa entertained her friends with the money Axel sent her for tuition, room and board. So Axel made arrangements with a local banker to pay Melissa's tuition and rent and to give her a small sum each week for food. Melissa and Philip were deeply at odds and had not spoken to each other for months. Philip was angry with Axel over how she dealt with Melissa.

It seemed to me that the case was very much about Melissa, so I asked, "Axel, what is the biggest problem in your life right now?"

"This thing with the chalet!" she exclaimed.

"Will solving the chalet problem solve the problem in your family?

"Well, no," she replied.

"How do you feel about what the builder did?"

"Ripped off!"

"And do you feel ripped off by your daughter?" I asked.

"Yes, but........."

Axel was near, but not in, the shaky zone. She did not want to see the truth, but the geographic and other curious connections between the chalet fiasco and the even bigger fiasco with her daughter were too compelling to ignore—as was the fact Axel had called me, perhaps the only lawyer in the United States who would explore her case in this way; as was the fact Melissa had recently changed her major from literature to *psychology*. Spirit does everything possible to get our attention.

I asked Axel to get back to me in a week or so because I felt there were other lessons in the case for her, but did not see what they were at the time. I also felt she had enough difficult material to consider for the time being. She said she would call me back the following week, but I never heard from her, and therefore cannot report how her case ended.

I often get into family dynamics when I work with people like Axel. Typically, the legal problem is only a symptom which diverts attention from the real issue, as in Axel's case. For her to deal with her lesson, she will have to do a very tough examination of her role as a mother and a wife. This will not be easy for Axel to do for it will entail her confronting Melissa's behavior which Axel has encouraged by continuing to *rescue* Melissa. My hunch is Melissa probably acts very much like Axel did when she was Melissa's age. It will also require Axel probing into why Melissa is so mad at her and Philip. Few parents care to do this sort of self-examination, and Axel is no exception. The next case demonstrates the wayward daughter drama from a different perspective.

The Woman Who Lost Her Child

Tracy's child was taken from her by Social Services. There were many facts supporting a charge of neglect, and a hearing had been set to terminate Tracy's parental rights. Tracy was a "flower child" (some would say, a "hippie") and lived most of the time in a van, traveling here and there with her friends. At twenty-seven, she had lived this way since she left home at age eighteen. She heard of my work and came to me for consultation. She was dressed in rags, and looked thin and tired. Her gentle look belied the inner turmoil.

"I want to find out what this is all about for me," she said.

"Fine," I said. "Where is your daughter now?"

"Social Services gave Amie to my parents until my case is heard."

"Where do they live?"

"In Minnesota."

"How do you feel about your parents having Amie?"

"Not very good."

"Why is that?"

"Well, they never were there for me, and I wonder

what it is like for Amie to be with them."

"What do you mean, they were never there for you?"

"Well, they provided a nice home, enough food, clothes and that sort of stuff, but they never provided love. They always told me how to live—what they wanted me to do when I grew up—that sort of stuff."

"And so you ran away?"

"Right. Just as soon as I felt old enough. I wanted to be free. Now I'm free of them. I do whatever I want."

"Well, they have Amie, don't they?"

"Well, yes."

"And you still don't like what they did to you growing up, do you?"

"No."

"The way you live now seems to be just the opposite of the way they live, yes?"

"That's right. They live in a cage. I live wherever I want to."

"So you are doing the opposite of what they did, right?"

"Right."

"And you gave Amie the opposite of what they gave you?'

"Right."

I suggested, far from being free, she was very much trapped in the past—that Amie was now with the very people she had run away from since she was eighteen.

It seemed her case was forcing her to face this old matter, as well as her reactionary life style. The court simply would not return Amie to her under the conditions in which she was then living. She did not want to deal with her parents, but she could not deny the situation with Amie was forcing her to do just that. We ended our meeting at this point, and she left. I did not hear from her afterwards, so I cannot report how this case turned out.

Tracy is not an unusual person. Like many young people, she "ran away from home" to get out from under the dominion of her parents. She left harboring deep resentment towards her parents. Her family situation was probably psychologically abusive. However, the fact that it was, or the fact that I might agree with her that it was, would not heal her wound. It would only have reinforced her ego belief that life was hopeless. The only thing that could have healed her was going home and walking "through the valley of the shadow of death." If she did, she began to heal. If she did not, she moved further into misery.

Mending our fences with our parents is not easy, but it is a lesson most of us are presented in life. If we do not learn it, then how can we help our children mend their fences with us—or ours with them? If Tracy mended her fences with her parents, that may have headed off her having a similar problem with Amie. The cycles repeat themselves, generation after generation, as the next case demonstrates.

Like Father, Like Son

Raymond came to me because of a boundary-line dispute. He and his father owned undeveloped land near the city. Adjacent to their land was a larger piece of land, owned by Mr. Smith and his son, Barry. The Smiths decided to develop their property, and had it surveyed. The survey revealed the fence everyone had assumed for decades to be the boundary was incorrect—that the true boundary was fifteen feet into the property Raymond and his father owned. Raymond heard of this, called Barry, and scheduled a face-to-face meeting on the property.

Mr. Smith met Raymond instead, and proceeded to curse him. Eventually, the matter ended up in court, and a drawn-out lawsuit ensued. It appeared Raymond would win on an adverse possession claim: the fence had been accepted as the true boundary by all owners in the chain of title for decades. Yet Mr. Smith said, "We will appeal this case if you win the trial. This will cost you a lot of money!" Raymond made many efforts to settle the case, but Mr. Smith rejected all offers.

I asked Raymond, had he been involved in any other lawsuits? He said he was involved in one he had filed against a local school system on behalf of his son several months before the boundary dispute arose. His son was seriously injured by a fall caused by another child pushing him off the jungle gym in the school playground one morning before school began. Raymond's father later brought over an agreement for his lawyer to sue the school system. Raymond signed the agreement, and his father's lawyer filed the lawsuit. I asked Raymond if he really believed the school system was responsible for his son's injuries?

"No," he said.

"So why did you sue them?" I asked.

"It was Dad's idea. He often sues people in his business.

I've never really felt right about him doing that—or this lawsuit against the school." he said.

I asked if he saw any similarity between his case against the school system and the one with the Smiths? He looked aghast. At that moment, he realized the Smiths reflected his relationship with his suit-happy father—that the boundary-line case was a rather crude suggestion that he needed to do something about his lawsuit against the school system. He saw that he would have to stand up to his father and stop the lawsuit. That troubled him because he had never been able to stand up to his father. He also realized Barry, not Mr Smith, was the key to resolving the boundary dispute, just as he (Raymond) was the key to resolving the suit against the school system. We ended the meeting, and Raymond left with much to think about.

A few months later he called to say he had dismissed the suit against the school system. Then his son remarkably improved. Raymond realized his son's slowness to heal had accommodated the needs of the lawsuit, which required serious injuries to be a potential money maker! That encouraged Raymond to talk with Barry. Unfortunately, no progress was made because Barry was not prepared to stand up to *his* father. The boundary-line case was still in progress as this book went to press.

We have a lawsuit mentality in this country, and Raymond's case demonstrates another reason for it. Raymond was courageous and broke the lawsuit cycle in his family. We will need many Raymonds to stop the rampant litigation swamping our courts and grinding justice to a halt. The next case demonstrates family patterns in a business law context.

The Corporation and the Black Widow Spider

This case involves Wyatt's manufacturing company. He and his managers use the hard-nosed, we-know-best, paternalistic management style. They are impatient with employee complaints, and, in fact, tend to resent them. They respond by stalling until the complainer gives up or quits—or by telling the complainer that he is damn lucky to have such a good job and is unappreciative and spoiled. An additional problem is Wyatt's alcoholism. Many of his managers are also alcoholics.

Recently, the employees got union representation. Wyatt and his managers were outraged: "What did we ever do to deserve this?" they complained. They spent a fortune on the best lawyers they could find in their losing attempt to defeat the union. I offered to share with Wyatt what I thought might be underlying his employee's dissatisfaction. He took a deep breath, and asked me to proceed. Here is the essence of what I told him.

A company is like a family with a similar personality. In this company family, there is no mother aspect. Children raised without a nurturing mother feel victimized. They are not happy. They complain a lot. The employees of a company are like children and need to be mothered, to counter-balance the tough fathering they receive. Because they are not being mothered, they react just as children do to such an imbalance. Furthermore, many of the employees had inadequate parenting when they were growing up. These employees are unconsciously reminded of their childhood unhappiness by the way management treats them. Thus, they react more strongly against the heavy-handed fathering management provides than one would expect without looking at the employees' family experiences.

Alcoholism adds to the problems. An alcoholic company is like an alcoholic family. Nothing works quite right in either. Employees of alcoholic businesses have troubles similar to children in alcoholic families—they feel extremely victimized. Employees harboring such feelings are not happy employees.

The union represents the unhealthy mother aspect. It promises to *rescue* the employees from the critical, dominating, demanding, alcoholic father, but like real mothers in alcoholic families, seldom delivers on its promises. The employees are desperate, and many of them embrace the union, even though it is probably a beautiful-but-deadly "black widow spider." The union officials feel the union has a good chance to get certified and they proceed towards certification. They win the certification election and experience a "honeymoon" with the employees. Later, the employees become unhappy with the union and turn their complaints against it. Such is the fate of the mother (rescuer) who does not succeed in rescuing her children from their overbearing, alcoholic father.

I believed Wyatt could prepare his company to oust the union by balancing a genuinely nurturing mother with a fair but demanding father in his company. By nurturing mother, I said I did not necessarily mean a woman manager, for in his company, such a change would be too radical. A man with a sensitive and loving nature could provide what was needed.

I also suggested that as long as Wyatt was an alcoholic and had alcoholic managers in his employ, it would matter very little what he did—that the problems would continue and even get worse, as they do in all alcoholic families. This was painful for Wyatt because he saw this was already happening: after the union was voted in, productivity declined, sales flattened, and profits declined.

Wyatt was not pleased to hear or see any of this, and I have not heard from him since I spoke to him.

Although I appreciate Wyatt's discomfort, I wonder how else he can cure his company's problems? Will he increase his advertising budget, cut the fat out of his company, hire a new plant manager, or find a buyer for his company? Will any of these symptomatic approaches solve his problems? When he dies, will God be impressed by his having taken any of these symptomatic approaches to curing the problems in his company?

The theme in Wyatt's company is seen in many businesses in America. Perhaps this explains why so many companies struggle with worker apathy, employee sabotage, absenteeism, alcoholism, and narcotics abuse? Perhaps this also explains why so many employees gripe and complain about their union after it becomes certified and doesn't rescue them from management like it promised it would?

Exercise

Take a moment to reflect on the material in this chapter. Do you see that what goes on in our families transfers into the legal arena? If so, what is it like for you to see this? What, if anything, are you going to do with this insight?

Legal problems start in our families, and expand from there to all areas of society. We need to start thinking about this. Proper parenting is important for children to grow. We need to love our children more, otherwise, we will continue to teach them to be like the people in this chapter.

Chapter Five

Conflict Law

This chapter links face-to-face conflict resolution to the big picture and introspective approaches to legal problems. I encourage my clients to use conflict resolution as part of a continuum, the third stage in resolving legal disputes. I prefer this three-tiered format because conflict resolution just does not reach as deeply as the other two approaches. However, I do not wish to slight conflict resolution because it can be a very effective soul-directed method of resolving legal wrangles in and of itself, and further because many legal conflicts must be outwardly faced and worked through, rather than avoided. Therefore, I will let conflict resolution stand on its own merits in this chapter.

Many people resist conflict resolution. There are many reasons for this resistance, and I will attempt to identify only three here. One is, it precludes winning a jackpot verdict and making off with an unconscionable amount of money. Another is, it causes disputants to resolve their differences, rather than fight like angry children or avenging victims. The third and perhaps most important reason for the resistance is, it scares many people out of their wits.

People instinctively approach conflict in one of two ways: first, by avoidance—running away, pretending everything is all right, or trying to make everyone involved happy; or second, by confrontation—blaming someone else or getting into a fight. This ego-instinctive flight-or-fight response is caused by two fears. The first fear is the ego fear of having to take responsibility for having consciously or unconsciously co-authored the conflict. This fear is tackled earlier, and I will not speak of it further here. The second fear arises out of having been threatened by our parents, relatives, and teachers with psychic or even physical harm if we honestly told them how we felt about the way they treated us. This is a deeper and more justifiable fear.

Most of us learned as children that being open and honest about our feelings was truly dangerous, so we developed a deep fear of saying how we felt about things. This fear, which is still in most of us, is activated by conflict. It is especially activated by conflict with another person who is important to us, say a spouse. That fear must be disarmed before conflict resolution can be successful. One way to disarm that fear is to understand and foresee the bad results which can come from not facing it.

Recall from Chapter 2 the cases about feigning forgiveness and turning the other cheek to avoid looking in the mirror. That is how many people covertly run from their fear of conflict. Other people do it more honestly: they simply run away, as the next few cases demonstrate.

The Docile Divorcee

I met Helen when I was buying insurance for my car. We talked about a lot of things. She asked what I did for a living, not an easy question to answer. I responded by telling her about this book which I was then writing.

"Have I got a case for you! " she said. "My husband Sam came home and out of the blue asked me for a divorce. I fell apart, then caved in to his demands during the divorce proceeding and signed the agreement his lawyer prepared. Sam got the house, the boat, his retirement plan, and I got the dog and had to go back to work. I never remarried, and after about five years contracted multiple sclerosis. One day, I got out our divorce agreement and read it for the first time since I signed it in my nice, sweet lawyer's office. When I saw what I had agreed to, I cried."

In every M.S. victim I have known, there is deep resentment towards self, or even an unconscious death wish—the ultimate self-destructive, unconscious thought of someone who hates self. I have discussed this with many spiritual "healers" and practitioners of "alternative medicine." They all agree: the body turns on itself to come into alignment with the person's attitudes towards self and life.

The "Friendly" Divorce

I met Carol at a party. During our talking, I told her I once practiced law, but now helped people try to understand their legal problems and respond to them in a different way. She said she had had a terrible experience, and wanted my advice. Here is what she said:

"Jack and I decided to get a divorce. He wanted to move out and buy a condominium. I would keep our home, but pay him for his share of the equity which he needed to close on the condominium. He said the equity in our home was $70,000. I was concerned about the real estate market and whether or not the home would clear $70,000 if I sold it. I wanted to investigate the value, but felt guilty about airing my concerns. I had seen many of my friends fight to the death in divorces, and I was determined that would not happen to me. I did not have the money to pay Jack, and did not have the income to put a larger mortgage on the home. So I went to my parents, who loaned me $35,000 to pay Jack. Six months after the divorce, I decided I would feel better living in a home in which Jack had not lived. I had several real estate brokers make proposals on the home. The selling prices they suggested would net only $50,000. I over-paid Jack $10,000 and am mad as hell at him."

Before she could ask what she should do, I asked, "Are you also mad as hell at yourself?" She looked at me and started crying.

The Man Who Felt Guilty

Will was referred to me by his business lawyer who did not handle domestic relations cases. Will's problem was that he was paying too much alimony to his first wife, and, as a result, his new family was in financial straits. The alimony amount had been set by agreement, voluntarily signed by Will. I asked him why had he had agreed to so much alimony, and he said, "I felt sorry for her, she was emotionally distraught, and I wanted to end it as peacefully as possible."

He said his ex-wife accused him of having an affair—that this led to the break-up of their marriage. He denied the affair, but I didn't believe him. His actions "circumstantially" proved his guilt, and he paid dearly for "buying" his way out. The only way he could get his alimony reduced was to show he had suffered a financial reversal. Remarrying was not considered a financial reversal by the courts in Alabama, and there was nothing I could do to help him.

Exercise

Take a few moments to think of the many people you know who caved in in a divorce case, only to rue it later. Did they ever forgive themselves? Are they still mad at their former spouse or their lawyer? What are their lives like? How is their physical and emotional health? How are their children doing?

As these cases suggest, it hurts us to turn our outer cheek when our inner cheek wants to fight but is afraid to do so. One of the most damaging things we can do to ourselves is to pretend to turn the other cheek when what we are really doing is running away. When we do this, we end up hating ourselves, and we turn our hatred inward.

So is it better to fight "like men?" We have seen in earlier chapters the damage which can be caused by taking the avenging approach. Rather than restate what was said there, I will share with you other cases which further demonstrate the risk inherent in that approach to conflict.

The Litigious Naturopath

This case involves Ian, who had much to do with my getting into this line of work. He is a naturopathic physician, skilled in acupuncture, homeopathy, and other forms of natural medicine. He received threatening letters from his state attorney general (at the urging of the state medical board) telling him to stop "practicing medicine" in his state. He met a lawyer who claimed to specialize in representing alternative physicians, and engaged this lawyer to file a huge anti-trust case against the state medical board. I was concerned about this lawyer's ethics and also about what this case would do to Ian and his family, and told him so. Had I known what I now know, I would have argued harder against his filing the lawsuit.

The lawyer filed the case, then became impossible to reach. A court hearing was set, the lawyer failed to show up, and the Judge dismissed the case for want of prosecution. Ian learned of this several weeks later. The lawyer attempted to get the case reinstated, but the judge would not reinstate it. The attorney general then sent Ian more threatening letters. Ian hired another lawyer, who filed a second case against the state medical board. This case was dismissed on the grounds that it was barred by the first case, which Ian had, in effect, lost. The judge ruled the second law suit was redundant, thus frivolous, and ordered Ian to pay the state medical board's lawyer fees. He gave up his rather expensive ideas about suing the medical board. Afterwards, he thought a lot about what Jesus said about suing people.

The I.U.D. Victim

Sabine became infertile by using an IUD which was later proven to be a health hazard. She hired a lawyer who filed a big lawsuit. Sabine was grilled by the defense lawyers in depositions and at the trial. The line of questioning went something like this.

"How old are you?

"Thirty seven."

"Are you married?"

"Yes."

"Is this your first marriage?"

"No. It's my third."

"How likely is it that you will have children?"

"Oh, pretty likely."

"Isn't it a little late for you to be thinking of having children?"

This line of questioning enraged the jury and won Sabine a big money award against the IUD manufacturer. If you were Sabine, how much money would you need to recover in this case to be healed? Would any amount of money heal you? Do you think Sabine is better off or worse off emotionally for having brought this case? Do you wonder if there is some connection between Sabine's infertility and her troubled relationships with men, which the defense attorney's questions hinted at? What do you suppose that connection might be? Was she aiming her resentment in the right direction?

The Daughter Who Died In the Boating Accident

Harry and Julie lost their nineteen-year-old daughter, Vanessa, in a boating accident. The boat was driven by Vanessa's boyfriend. He was on drugs and lost control of the boat, flipping it several times at high speed. Both were killed. Harry and Julie filed a lawsuit against the boyfriend's estate. The case was defended by the insurance company which had written the liability policy on the boat. At the trial, the insurance company's lawyers defended the case by proving Vanessa knew her boyfriend was a drug user and was using drugs just prior to getting into the boat. This was very painful for Harry and Julie because it was true. The truth indirectly cast the blame for the matter onto Harry and Julie for not raising their daughter to exercise better judgment. The jury decided Vanessa assumed the risk and ruled against her parents. Do you think Harry and Julie are better or worse off for having brought this case? Did the lawsuit divert them from facing how they feel towards Vanessa, towards themselves for how they raised her, or towards God for taking their daughter? If so, will they ever heal their loss?

The Nasty Divorce

Rather than relate a case to you, I invite you to take a few moments to think of one or two nasty divorce and child custody cases which have affected you or people you know. If you cannot think of any such cases, then you are, indeed, an unusual and most fortunate person. As a lawyer, I handled many divorce cases. Most of these cases settled before trial, but they were nevertheless quite heated. The spouses yelled at and threatened each other, directly and through their lawyers—and through their children. The entire family was gravely damaged by this, and the damage showed up in emotional disturbances and physical complaints that will, in many cases, plague them the rest of their lives.

The spouses knew they were damaging themselves and their children, but could not help themselves. I felt powerless to stop the carnage. Now when I work with parents who are in conflict, I always share with them the stories about my son's death and Nelle's later accident which occurred to correct the many unresolved problems that lingered after her brother's death. That causes my clients to catch their breath. I leave the rest to Spirit.

The Texas Massacre

A far-reaching legal fiasco was the *Pennzoil v. Texaco* case. Pennzoil had a verbal agreement to buy Getty Oil Company, and Texaco induced Getty to sell to Texaco instead. Pennzoil proposed negotiations, and Texaco and its lawyers ignored Pennzoil's offers to negotiate. Pennzoil filed a 3.3 billion dollar lawsuit, tried in Houston, Texas, Pennzoil's home town, under Texas law. After Pennzoil presented its side of the story, Texaco arrogantly refused to put on any evidence. The jury returned a verdict for 3.3 billion dollars, which was trebled to 10 billion dollars under the Texas anti-trust statute

Texaco was forced to file for protection under the federal bankruptcy laws. Ultimately, the case was settled for 3 billion dollars. The lawyers made outrageous fees. A major U.S. corporation was critically damaged. Thousands of Texaco employees were hurt by their company's reduced capacity to increase salaries, wages or benefits, or make contributions to the employee pension and profit sharing plans. Thousands of Texaco stock and bond holders suffered securities losses, as Texaco's stock and credit rating went down. Stock brokers, stock arbitrageurs, and professional investors made fortunes, as investors traded Pennzoil and Texaco stock back and forth.

This case was insane, as are most legal battles. Pennzoil would probably have settled this case up front for 500 million dollars, or less. Texaco paid dearly for its arrogance. This case should be taken as a major lesson by this country. It represents the ultimate disastrous result of the hateful attitude so many people take into conflict. What does this case tell us about ourselves? How does the result transfer into improving the health of our nation's businesses? What do our children learn to be like when they see things such as this being reported on television? That the way to solve their problems is to win a big lawsuit? Will Pennzoil's extreme recovery make all unhappy people hope for a jack-pot verdict? If so, reasonable and fair settlements will be even more difficult to achieve.

Not all fight-to-the-death cases are tried. In fact, most are settled using self-interest (adversarial) bargaining. In the self-interest approach, people view the other side as being the problem. Finger-pointing, blaming, and name-calling are part of the game plan, as are stalling, bluffing, threatening, lying, and cheating—whatever it takes to win. This is how many people approach conflict. After it's over, they are the worse for wear.

Cases which settle from self-interest bargaining often have worse results than those tried to the death. The posturing and finger-pointing leading up to the actual settlement end with both sides being enraged; then the settlement stops the case without either side getting a chance to express their resentment. They get a lukewarm settlement which their lawyer has advised them to take — and a belly-full of bad feelings. They hate the other side (and themselves for settling), and often project this hate onto their lawyer, claiming he sold them out. This underlies most of the settlement complaints lawyers so often hear: the parties leave without dealing with their feelings.

Many lawyers prefer self-interest bargaining to mutual-interest-based conflict resolution. There are two principle reasons for this. The first is, mutual-interest-based conflict resolution is not always appropriate. This problem is explored towards the end of this chapter. The second reason is, lawyers don't make much money when the parties try to work out their differences peacefully. Those issues aside, the important question is: how do the results of mutual-interest-based conflict resolution compare to the results achieved in self-interest bargaining? During the mediation training I took at the Center for Dispute Resolution (now known as CDR & Associates) in Boulder, Colorado, one of the trainers spoke to this concern.

This instructor said, "The research to date shows little difference in the size of legal settlements using the two approaches. What the research has shown is this: in self-interest bargaining, the parties almost always go away mad as hell, whereas in mutual-interest-based conflict resolution, they usually do not. In fact, they usually part with a much better understanding of and appreciation for the other side."

Before giving mutual-interest-based conflict resolution examples, I will first share several cases in which a mutual-interest-based result was achieved through what can best be described as "spiritual intervention."

The Chastened Naturopath

I reported earlier in this chapter Ian's difficulties with suing the state medical board. It wasn't long before the attorney general filed a cease-and-desist action against Ian, asking the court to order him to stop practicing medicine. This re-opened the door for Ian to raise the anti-trust charges as a defense, but not as an attack. Even so, that defense would have required him to make accusations of wrongdoing by the medical board. He chose, instead, to simply ask the court to determine whether or not his work was illegal, and offered to close his practice if the court decided it was.

This approach impressed the judge. He found what Ian did was not taught in the state medical schools and was not practiced by licensed physicians in that state. Nor did the state medical board allow physicians to do what Ian did. Therefore, Ian's work was something other than the practice of medicine. The judge nevertheless felt Ian's work should be supervised by a physician, and ruled as long as he was supervised by an M.D., an osteopath, or a chiropractor, he could continue his work. By chance (if you believe in chance), Ian had recently employed a chiropractor in his office, and meeting the judge's requirement was a simple matter. The coincidence did not go unnoticed and Ian's belief in God was strengthened because of it.

The Paraplegic Woman

Agnes, a professional athlete, was rendered paraplegic in an automobile accident and filed a lawsuit against the driver of the other car who was at fault. She was enraged. She came to Dr. John Upledger who was able to help her up to a point, but there was so much damage it soon became clear to him she would never walk again. "She rejected my prognosis and, in fact, became very angry over it," John said to me. "She was angry at everything, even God."

Over time, Agnes was forced by her condition to find another way of earning a living. She began working with injured people in John's clinic, and became excellent at helping these people put their injuries behind them and get on with their lives. Yet she held onto the hope that she would make a full recovery.

One day, she had the startling realization that, if she were to recover, then she would no longer be able to do the work she was doing. The fact that she was herself crippled and was getting on with her life was the key to her effectiveness. The people in the clinic could not argue with her because she was a living example of what she taught. She saw that she had discovered her life's work—that but for the accident this would not have occurred. She forgave the driver who injured her, and settled the lawsuit. Although she would never walk again, she could fly.

The Mayhem Victim

Linda was unexpectedly attacked by a crazed woman who came running up to her car screaming for help. Linda said, "I rolled down my window and tried to talk with the woman, who grabbed my left hand and screamed, 'If you don't give me the keys to your car, I will kill you!' I tried to free my hand, and the woman bit my left ring finger and held onto it like a bulldog. After what seemed like forever, I was able to free my hand and roll up the window. The police came and arrested the woman. I nearly lost my finger. I struggled with what to do, and decided to sign a warrant charging the woman with mayhem.

"I was terrified of what would happen if I went through with the prosecution. I went to my spiritual mentor who said that I had long suffered from a fear of a violent death at the hands of a man and that fear was at the root of my never having married. This case brought these matters to my attention.

"A court hearing was set and I went to it with my lawyer, the district attorney, the defendant, her lawyer, and her probation officer. I asked why she attacked me, and she said her husband was addicted to drugs and alcohol and had beaten her for several weeks. Just before the incident, he threatened to kill her, and she fled for her life—out of her mind. She attacked me, she said, because she had to get rid of her feelings.

"The probation officer confirmed the woman's story. I realized we shared similar fears of a violent death at the hands of men, and I cried. I told her I understood and could forgive her, and we hugged. About a year later, I met my husband."

Linda's assailant reflected what Linda needed to face. Linda got the message and began to look at her fear. Had she focused on punishing her assailant, she would only have made matters worse for herself. How do you think Linda's lesson would have been packaged the next time?

The Woman Whose Husband Was Unfaithful

I learned of Dolly's story from Allen, her lawyer, and requested permission to talk with her. Allen called her, and she agreed to talk with me. We met for lunch, and I found her to be an exuberant and delightful middle-age woman. She was pleased to share her case with me, and I will relate it to you in her words as I remember them.

"I discovered Terrance was having an affair with a much younger woman," she said. "I confronted him with it, he confessed, and, much to my distress, they moved into an apartment together. I went to Allen who goes to my church and asked for his help. He asked if I still loved Terrance, and I said I did and did not want a divorce. Allen suggested I take a wait-and-see approach. I was torn as to what to do. I still loved Terrance but felt very hurt and angry. I told Allen I would give it a try."

"Every two or three weeks I called Allen, and each time he told me to keep waiting. This went on for several months. I went through all sorts of violent emotions during this time. I yelled and screamed at Allen, at God, and at my friends. I woke up terrified and crying more times than I can remember. I was terrified of living alone. This went on for weeks. Then I began to see things about myself I did not particularly want to see. It was hard. Then Terrance called to say he wanted to move back in, but wanted to keep his apartment and girlfriend. I called Allen and asked him what to do. He told me to tell Terrance he could come back after he gave up the apartment and girlfriend, which I did."

"Several weeks later, Terrance came by and said he wanted to give up his girlfriend and the apartment, and come home. He asked for forgiveness. I told him I felt he was not completely at fault—that I had done things which contributed to the problem. He cried. Then I cried. We cried a long time together. Our relationship is much better than it was before all of this happened."

Had Dolly not been able to follow Allen's advice, she would have been traumatized by a nasty divorce proceeding, lost the man she loved, and harbored resentment towards him (and towards herself) for the rest of her life. Instead, she followed her soul's guidance, put herself in the shaky zone, and opened to healing. In doing so, she transformed herself and her marriage as well.

As Dolly's case suggests, there are times when it is best to back off from an immediate confrontation and take a wait-and-see approach. Here is another case in which that method worked out well.

California Bound

Mike is a quiet, solid-looking man in his late thirties. He visited in my home and learned of this book I was writing. I said I needed cases which demonstrated "yielding" in legal disputes. His eyes sparkled, as he said he had one he wanted to share with me:

"I have a son, Josh, by my first wife, Nan," he said. "Nan and I have a joint custody agreement which provides for Josh to live every other month with me and every other month with her. Nan took a notion to move to California, and Josh said he wanted to go. I thought it was a terrible idea, but could not talk them out of it. So I just told them to go. It tore me up inside, but I knew a court fight would tear me up more, and Josh would be mad at me. Anyway, they went. Nan never found what she was looking for out there. They lived in four different places in a year's time, and then they came back. Josh was so glad to be back that he could not wait to come live with me. Nan was more than happy for him to do this."

Had Mike resisted Nan or Josh, they would have fought back. It would not have mattered who won. There would have been hard feelings from Nan and Josh toward Mike, and hard feelings from him toward them. This painful result was avoided by Mike's decision to yield and wait. Now Josh lives with him, and they enjoy their relationship. Here is a similar case in which yielding paid big dividends.

Avoiding Solomon's Choice

Bobbie decided to ask her husband, Jack, a tough trial lawyer, for a divorce. He reacted by threatening to fight for full custody of their daughter, Susie, even though he spent only a short time with her each week. Bobbie was interested in metaphysics and natural health-care, which bewildered the conservative Jack. Bobbie was afraid her interests would bewilder the local judges, as well, and given Jack's connections with them, she had good reason to be concerned. She came to me for advice. I advised her to be careful about giving in, as she would probably hate Jack and herself, hate she would probably spew onto him and their daughter for years. She thanked me and left.

I saw Bobbie at church a few weeks later. I asked her what happened? She smiled, then said, "I went to our minister and told him what was happening. He advised me to offer full custody to Jack. I nearly choked at the thought. Then I prayed on the matter and did just that. Jack really did choke, for there was no way he could take on the full responsibility of raising Susie and still practice law. So, we agreed to joint custody. I was able to pursue other interests which I had been putting off, and Jack, bless his heart, spends a lot more time with Susie, which benefits them both."

Had Bobbie played the victim and chosen to fight with Jack, there would have been a nasty child-custody fight, with wrenching psychological evaluations, invasive cross-examination by each other's lawyer, and painful testimony by both sets of grandparents. The discord would have left lasting emotional scars in everyone concerned.

The Spiritual Family

Victor and Zoe were in the throes of a divorce. Their marriage failed because Victor became a Christian and Zoe remained Jewish. Both were sincere in their beliefs, and both respected the other's sincerity. However, neither was able to embrace the other's religion, and neither wanted their children, Alice and Arnie, to be influenced by the other's religion. Judges have to decide such matters when the parents are not in agreement, and that is where the case was headed. Then Zoe dreamed she was in court where the case was tried:

"I was in the courtroom," she said. "My lawyer was beside me. Victor was there with his lawyer. Alice and Arnie sat where the judge sits. Both wore black judge's robes. Between them sat Jesus, also in a black judge's robe. Jesus said, 'We have reached a decision. Please stand.' We all stood, and Jesus said, 'Alice and Arnie chose both of you to be their parents, and both of you agreed to be their parents. They have important things to learn from you, and you have important things to learn from them. Therefore, they shall be both Christians and Jews, and you shall teach them these things.' I shared my dream with Victor, and we sat down and cried together. We are now teaching Alice and Arnie both religions."

Spirit directly intervened in this case. It's too bad this sort of thing does not happen more often in child custody cases in which parents truly destroy themselves and their children.

Now let's carry the impressions and results from these exceptional cases into mutual-interest-based conflict resolution, which in legal circles is called "third-party mediation," or simply "mediation."

In mediation, the problem is treated as being mutual and capable of resolution. A neutral third person helps us work things out. Finger-pointing, blaming, and name-calling are not permitted because that only drives us apart. When you are talking, I am not allowed to interrupt—and vice versa. This causes me to hear you out, and you to hear me out. For many people, being listened-to is a brand new experience, and for others, being quiet while someone else is talking is a new experience. Would either be a new experience for people you know? For you?

Let's explore how the *Pennzoil v. Texaco* case might have turned out in mediation.

Averting the Massacre

What if Pennzoil's CEO, whom I will call "Mr. Penn," called Texaco's CEO, whom I will call "Mr. Tex."

Suppose Mr. Penn said, "Hey, we already have a contract with Getty! Don't you know about it?"

Suppose Mr. Tex said, "I know you made a gentlemen's agreement, but we do not feel it's legally binding on Getty, and Getty likes our offer better."

Then suppose Mr. Penn said, "It seems Getty's playing us off against each other. Perhaps she should be made to pay for that?"

Mr. Tex might respond, "Yeah, she's being fickle isn't she?"

Mr. Penn might say, "Well, we can't both buy Getty, can we?"

Mr. Tex would say, "Of course not."

Mr. Penn might say, "Why don't we get someone we both trust to help us work this out. If we can't resolve it that way, then we can do battle."

Mr. Tex might then say, "Well, if we can work this out peacefully, that would sure be better than launching legal missiles at each other in court, wouldn't it? Boy, my lawyers sure won't like me doing this. Well, that's their problem!"

Then Mr. Penn and Mr. Tex meet with a mediator. The mediator first lays some ground rules. One of the rules is, it is the mediator's job to help reach an agreement which is good for both. Another is, no blaming of the other side. A third is, when one side is talking, the other has to be quiet. Then the mediator lets one side tell its story about the purchase of Getty, and then the other side.

As Mr. Penn and Mr. Tex talk, the mediator writes down the common issues and areas of agreement, such as: Getty is having a lot of fun at their expense; Pennzoil could have avoided this by putting its agreement in writing; Texaco could have avoided this by waiting; a lawsuit will cost both sides millions of dollars in legal expenses; both companies' stocks and bonds will be the subject of mass speculation; the case will take much of the time and energy of top management; the loser will pay dearly on Wall Street. Therefore, it is better to work out a mutual solution which avoids those hazards. (The actual preliminary agreement would be rather long, and is found in Appendix "A" at the end of the book.)

After this meeting, Mr. Tex calls the CEO of Getty and says that Texaco fears being sued by Pennzoil and that Getty will have to clear up Pennzoil's claim before Texaco can buy Getty. Getty's CEO calls Mr. Penn, makes an offer, and is rebuffed. Getty is in a pickle, one it rightly deserves to be in. Its tongue is hanging out, thinking about all that money getting away. It invites Texaco and Pennzoil to a three-way meeting, and there proposes to reduce its selling price and pay the reduction to Pennzoil. After fierce negotiations between Mr. Tex and Mr. Penn accompanied by name-calling, dire threats, and counter threats (all staged for Getty's benefit), Getty reduces its price much further. Pennzoil says it is satisfied, and Texaco closes the deal and later settles up with Pennzoil. Getty gets a fair, instead of an outrageous, price. Texaco and Pennzoil—and their employees and securities holders—come out way ahead. The Wall Street Journal and other publications report a much different story, one that teaches Americans an entirely new way of resolving conflict.

How does that scenario feel to you? Does this outcome seem better than Pennzoil and Texaco trying to destroy each other? Do you think Pennzoil would have taken this approach before it knew what the jury verdict would be? Do you think Texaco now wishes it had? Do you think this is a better outcome than the actual result? Do you ever see people resolving their legal wrangles this way? Such dispute resolutions can only be reached by people who are interested in healing their differences—people who are not afraid to face conflict openly and honestly—people who are tired of being victims. In other words, by adults.

A Healing Divorce

Let's look at one more mediation case. This one involves a bitter divorce. Janet and Peter were really going at each other, and their two children were being hurt emotionally. Janet frightened the children by drinking too much, cursing Peter, and telling the children their father was going to put them in the poor house. She would not allow him to see the children except when she needed a break. Peter had a new girlfriend, and Janet would not allow him to see the children when the girlfriend was around. Peter was enraged because Janet used their credit cards up to their limits after he moved out. She bought a new wardrobe and took an expensive vacation with some of her girlfriends, leaving him with the children at a time when he had conflicting business plans. Janet often left the children with baby sitters and came home after they were asleep. Peter was worried about her emotional stability and was considering fighting for sole custody.

Sound familiar? There is a lot of victim-like behavior going on here. This is a fairly typical divorce case. How are they usually resolved? If you haven't lived through this first hand, then ask your friends. You probably have plenty of them who have been through this. Here is how a mediator might work with this couple from a spiritual perspective. Not all mediators work this way. I propose they should.

The mediator first meets with Janet and Peter separately to create a relationship with each of them, to learn about the case from each point of view, and to explain and get agreement on the ground rules: no name-calling, blaming, interrupting, or withholding important information. Both Janet and Peter are gripped with fear, and on the verge of fleeing or fighting. Any form of attack by one on the other (or by the mediator on either of them) will trigger the flight-or-fight response in the one attacked. That will hurt or even destroy the chances of reaching an agreement. This should be explained by the mediator to each of them separately. Otherwise, each is likely to launch a first-strike attack.

To help Janet and Peter understand the importance of not attacking each other, the mediator demonstrates to them how it feels to hear attacking words. Let's assume the mediator is with Peter. The mediator suggests an "experiment" in which Peter will tell the mediator, "It's all your fault!" Peter may be reluctant to say this to the mediator because he knows such words usually evoke a counter-attack. The object is to help Peter to see how these words affect him. So it is not important that he actually say the words to the mediator. It is okay if he does, as long as he does it willingly. Nothing should be forced in mediation. Forcing only causes people to feel victimized and makes them angry and resistant.

Then the mediator asks Peter if the experiment can be reversed, "just to see what we can learn." Again, it is not important that Peter agree to participate. Whether or not the mediator says the words to Peter, he will get the point. The mediator and Peter talk about how awful it feels to be blamed for something. Then the mediator asks, "Do you think Janet feels the way we do about this?" Peter will most likely agree.

Next the mediator demonstrates to Peter the difference between attacking and making an overture towards a peaceful resolution. The mediator suggests another experiment. In this experiment, the mediator asks Peter what he feels when he hears these words: "I am sorry about this problem between us and for what I have done to create it." Peter will notice he likes hearing these words. The mediator probably gets Peter to admit at this point that Janet will also like hearing these words. Peter agrees to say this to Janet early in the three-way meeting which will later occur. The mediator also goes through a similar process with Janet to prepare her for the three-way meeting.

The mediator then meets with Janet and Peter together. The mediator helps Janet and Peter express their pent-up feelings without attacking each other. For example, Janet might have been coached in her private meeting with the mediator to say, "I feel awful when I think about you sleeping with your new girlfriend, especially around our children," instead of, "You lying, cheating bastard!" Peter might have been coached to say, "Using up the credit card limits really made me mad," instead of, "You vindictive bitch; I'll never give you another cent!"

The mediator then guides Janet and Peter towards saying what worries them. For example, Janet might have been coached say, "I am afraid for my financial security." Peter is not allowed to reply, "You are getting what you deserve!"

Or Peter might have been coached to say, "I am concerned about where all the money will come from." Janet is not allowed to reply, "You lout, you want to put us in the poor house!"

Finally, the mediator penetrates what is really going on about the children. Although Janet's behavior is frightening, it is not unusual for a mother to act this way during a divorce. Most likely, Janet is lost and despairing, and will calm down. Husbands (and their lawyers) often focus on the wife's grief to support custody claims being made "to protect the children." Wives do this, too, when the husband is grieving during a divorce, to limit the father's visitation so as "to protect the children." Underneath this smoke-screen is something vital.

Janet and Peter are using their children to express the conscious rage they feel towards each other, and to express the unconscious rage they feel towards themselves and all of the other people in their lives who have hurt them. They are also using their children to replace the companionship they once had with each other. It is important to understand that Janet and Peter are not acting as loving as they would in less stressful circumstances. Most (if not all) of their unresolved psychological and spiritual problems are being raised at this time, and they are terrified. But this is the best they can do for the time being. If either feels blamed, the other will fight back. So the mediator approaches the storm indirectly. Here's how it might be done in this case.

The mediator helps Janet and Peter to agree to as many things as possible about the children: the parents both love their children; they both want to be thought of as being good parents; both want what is best for their children; their children will be better off if they are not directly involved in their parents' disagreements, and if their parents are able to get along with each other; the less disruptive for the children the divorce is, the better off all will be afterwards; and finally, the children's needs are at least as important as the parents' needs. This may cause a radical change in Janet and Peter, as they begin to see what is really important here. Such a realization reached from within has much more chance of effecting change than does a direct confrontation. In fact, a direct confrontation has almost no chance of working. The ego cannot take such an onslaught under this much stress.

Once the mediator has Janet and Peter in alignment about the children, the way is paved towards working out an initial agreement. (That agreement might look like the one set out in Appendix "B".) Many of the immediate concerns and hard feelings have now been faced. There is an opportunity for real healing to occur. To further that healing, the mediator gives Janet and Peter an exercise to do before the next three-way meeting. He asks each of them to make a list of the things they like about each other. The list is to be made over time, with items being added to it as they come to mind. The list is not to be shared, unless both Janet and Peter wish to do this. Requiring that the list be shared might be a turn-off.

This is a vital step in healing their hatred of each other, and thus of the opposite sex. As Janet and Peter do this exercise, they will slowly make a list of beautiful things they see in each other—and indirectly in themselves. They will start to feel better about each other (and the opposite sex), and about themselves. By the time they meet again, they will feel much differently toward each other, the opposite sex, and themselves. They may even be open to reconciliation. If not, they may at least part in peace. If they do not part in peace, they will carry their opposite-sex hatred and self-hatred into their next relationships, and the cycles will repeat.

Should either Janet or Peter withdraw from mediation and let their lawyers fight it out, the outcome will probably be about the same as that achieved through mediation. However, that result will be achieved through hurtful, self-interest bargaining, or imposed in a year or two by a judge, with Janet and Peter having no control over the outcome. A couple of lawyers will make a bundle. Very likely, the case will be taken back to court within the next couple of years. Statistics show this seldom happens when the spouses sit down and talk.

Exercise

Take a moment to reflect on this mediation example. What are you experiencing as a result of having read this material? How does the result suggested in this example compare with the results you have seen in divorce cases? Which result do you like best?

The glowing picture just painted is not an unconditional recommendation for mediation. There are cases when it is clearly not appropriate, several examples of which are reported in the next chapter. Sometimes mediation appears to be appropriate, when actually it is inappropriate. This is a dangerous area, and I will share a few of these types of cases with you, so you can avoid the trap the people in these cases fell into.

The Power Struggle

Beverly agreed in mediation to a joint custody arrangement under which her son, Bobby, lived half the time with his father, Jack, and all major decisions about Bobby had to be made jointly.

Beverly told me, "It's a real pain in the neck having to go to Jack every time I need to make an important decision. He almost always does not agree with me. I think he does it to get even with me, not because he is concerned about Bobby. For instance, Bobby has signs of hyperactivity and learning disorders. He needs close supervision. His public school teachers are pressuring me to put him on ritalin. I know a small, private school with a lower student-teacher ratio would help Bobby. If things keep going as they are, he will end up with some very serious problems. My hands are tied. No court would order Jack to allow Bobby to go to private school, at least not without a lot of psychological testimony, which costs a fortune to get and probably would damage Bobby even further."

Many mediators promote joint custody agreements because they think this is the "right" way for divorcing parents to deal with their children. Often this is how the mediators handled their own divorces. Judges in Birmingham, Alabama experimented with joint custody in the early 1980's and found joint decision-making agreements were far more trouble than they were worth—that a disproportionately high percentage of such agreements were brought back to court for judicial refereeing. The judges found, far from resolving their differences, the parents had merely postponed the fight. The parents thought they did the "right" thing by agreeing to joint decision-making. In reality, they ran away from their fear of openly and honestly tackling the problems which later surfaced.

The Slippery Father

In another case, Jennifer attempted to mediate her divorce with her husband, Jeff. They worked out custody, but Jeff would not agree to a reasonable amount of child support. So they agreed to the custody part and further agreed to let the judge decide the amount of support. The judge awarded Jennifer a greater amount of child support than she had requested in the mediation process. Jeff "lost" his job and began earning money underground. His earnings could not be proven. The judge would not do anything to him. The custody could not be changed, as custody and support are not linked by the courts in divorce cases. By mediating custody, Jennifer lost her bargaining power on the support issue.

"I made a big mistake, mediating with Jeff," she said.

Mediators tend to be biased towards getting the parties to reach an agreement, at least in part. When they force an agreement, cases such as Jennifer's result. Jeff did not mediate in good faith, and the mediator did not handle this. The mediator should have suggested that perhaps mediation was not appropriate for Jennifer and Jeff. The mediator should have pointed out the risks involved in a piece-meal agreement. This would have brought the risks into the open and given Jennifer an opportunity to decide, based on all the facts, whether or not to proceed with mediation.

The Boy Next Door

In another case, an adolescent girl had sex with the boy next door. Her parents reacted as avenging victims and took her to a mediator to get her to agree not to see the boy anymore. Her parents also wanted to rearrange her life (by setting curfews, etc.), which had previously been fairly unrestricted. Actually, the girl matured early because her parents were never around. The mediator had a daughter of his own and sided with the parents, and so a one-sided agreement was reached, which the girl signed, thinking she had no other choice. She broke the agreement in two days.

Mediators often have children of their own, which can affect their neutrality. The mediator in this case was biased and sided with the parents. The girl was wrongfully blamed twice: for acting as an adult, as her parents had raised her to be; and for breaking an unfair agreement. Her first experience with sex was turned into a nightmare. There is no telling how much psychological damage she will have as the result of this mediation. Will this experience result in her adopting a victim attitude towards life? Becoming promiscuous to get even with her parents? Becoming frigid, to atone for her ways? Using drugs to ease her pain?

It is not appropriate to mediate a settlement which sets up a later power struggle, as in Beverly's case. It is not appropriate to mediate when the other side is not mediating in good faith, as in Jennifer's case. It is not appropriate to mediate when the real purpose of the mediation is to control and blame another person, and thus deny our own error, as in this last case.

Exercise

Take a moment to reflect on the material in this chapter. What are you feeling after reading it? Do you have a different understanding of the fear underlying legal conflict and how this fear causes people to either flee or fight? Do you have a different view towards conflict resolution and why it is so important? If you are a lawyer, do you have a better understanding of mediation and the damage being caused by clients resolving their legal disputes through self-interest bargaining and lawsuits? Are you more open to exploring mediation as a way of resolving legal disputes?

Most people resist mutual-interest-based conflict resolution because they are terrified of conflict. This terror is rooted in two things: unwillingness to take responsibility for having helped create the difficulty, and childhood experiences in which we learned it was not safe to openly and honestly express our feelings. Legal conflict is an opportunity to heal by taking responsibility for having contributed to the problem, by openly and honestly expressing our fears and concerns without attacking—or being attacked by—the other side, and by finding solutions which work for both sides. Then we can move ahead in our lives, rather than backwards.

Chapter Six

True Justice

This chapter is about what to do if we have no choice but to go to court. We have all seen people who never take responsibility for their mistakes or admit wrongdoing. They represent the hard-core elements in our society who feel the most victimized by life—the most separated from God within and without. They often act out their terror and rage by legal wrongdoing. They are so damaged that they cannot see the big picture, use introspection, or join us in mediation. If they did, the terror and rage they might feel would overwhelm them, perhaps drive them insane. Such people must be dealt with by gross measures, such as lawsuits and criminal prosecutions. These are the only ways we can manage them and protect ourselves from them.

We need to be very careful when we seek "justice." Far too many people say they seek it, when what they really seek is vindication and revenge—an eye for an eye, a tooth for a tooth. Jesus advised against that approach to law enforcement, one far more prevalent in this country than in any other predominately Christian country. Try as I might, I cannot understand how Christians support some of the aspects of our legal system, especially capital punishment, the ultimate expression of vengeance, which violates the Commandment, "Thou shalt not kill," and disregards Jesus's teachings about loving and forgiving our enemies.

Capital punishment does not undo what has been done. It does not cause repentance. It does deprive the criminal of the opportunity to repent and reconnect with God, which result is the ultimate "cruel and unusual punishment." Life imprisonment without parole in a maximum security facility takes the offender out of circulation, but leaves an opportunity for introspection and healing. Providing that opportunity to capital offenders is the ultimate expression of compassion, a word the avenging ego does not understand.

The avenging ego seeks vindication and revenge, calling that "justice." True justice, on the other hand, is dispassionate. It is impartial. It is necessary. It has nothing to do with proving that we are right or getting revenge. People who break the law need to be dealt with so they will not create further harm to people or to society. They need to be taken out of circulation. Perhaps they even need to be sterilized, so they will not create more people like them. In this way, we send a message to all that we will deal similarly with them if they break our laws. However, it is not our proper role to be the final judge of human behavior. That is God's role, one we all too often usurp.

Another aspect of true justice is, it can only be achieved by finding and honoring "the truth, the whole truth, and nothing but the truth." Few people really want to see the whole truth when it does not give them what they want. Such people are as selfish, as deeply stuck in ego denial, and as damaged as the people whom they wish to correct or punish. Such people can be described as being "self-righteous" or having "righteous indignation."

Often they are as guilty in their hearts as the criminals they seek to punish are in the flesh.

Proponents of capital punishment are such people. They never physically murdered or raped any body, but they psychically murdered and raped a lot of people. They support unconscionable wars like the one in Viet Nam, thus murdering Americans and citizens of other countries alike. They defend private ownership of semi-automatic rifles and thereby make such weapons available to murderers. Most likely they kill their fair share of animals. They rape mother nature by littering and by dumping toxic chemicals on her. And they probably were psychically murdered and raped when they were children, the same as the criminals they wish to put to death. Murder and rape must be viewed in this broader context if we are to understand what fuels the thirst for capital punishment.

Jimmy Bakker represents an extreme example of the incorrigible spiritual law breaker who attacks what is "out there" to avoid facing what is "in here." Bakker saw (and perhaps still sees) Satan everywhere but in himself, and used that way of thinking to bilk similarly fearful people out of millions of dollars. The interesting thing is, Bakker really believed he was innocent of wrong-doing: he really believed he did God's work. That's how damaged he was, and his wife and followers were just as damaged—just as disconnected from God as Bakker.

Bakker preached, Jesus, but did not understand him. Jesus demonstrated during the three temptations that Satan is inside, not outside. Jesus never described Satan as being a bearded, horned, arrowhead-tailed, cloven-footed, red beast, holding a pitchfork: Dante did that. Jesus described Satan as his own human weakness—his own ego. Jesus apparently had the power to perform miracles, to rule the world, and to save himself from his enemies. His ego wanted to do that. He wrestled with that temptation, and prevailed. In doing so, he moved closer to his Divine nature. That is what Bakker and people like him need to do—to find and wrestle the Satan in themselves.

It is similar with people like Zsa Zsa Gabor. Gabor hates Nazis, and policemen remind her of the Gestapo, and ultimately of her male God. When she was tried for assaulting a police officer, she said America was a worse police state than Hitler's Germany. Does Gabor look in the right place for Nazis? Should she be looking in the mirror instead? Should she be looking at her relationship with a Nazi-like image of God?

Gabor reminds me of Josie, a young Jewish woman who came to me. Josie was having recurring nightmares about being assaulted and raped by Nazis. She hated men and was an active Zionist. I asked her to allow the Nazis in her dreams to come into her imagination. Then I asked her to let them select one Nazi to represent all. She described a huge, bearded, Attila-the-Hun-like thug who stepped forward to be the representative. I asked her to watch Attila as I spoke to him.

"Attila," I said, "I am going to say something to you, and I want you to decide what, if anything, you will do in response to what I say." I paused a moment, then said, "Show her who you really are." Josie nearly jumped out of her chair. "What happened?" I asked.

"I can't believe it!" she exclaimed.

"Can't believe what?"

"He became me! I was looking at myself!"

That experience allowed her to look at how she behaved like a Nazi. She was able to accept the Attila in herself. Her Nazi dreams stopped. She lost her zeal for Jewish causes, and turned her attention to things she really enjoyed: gardening, sewing, walking in the woods, and making love with her new, Gentile boyfriend.

My hunch is that Gabor will never rid herself of her fear of Nazis by the course she takes. What if there were no more policemen? Would that satisfy her? Or would she find some other outer symbol to represent Nazis and her hatred of God? And what about the other side: the people who hate Jews, Negroes, etc.? Are they any different from Gabor? Do they see themselves in Jews, Negroes, and other minorities, and hate what they see? I ask those people this question: If they got rid of all of the Jews, Negroes, and other minority groups they do not like, would they be happy? Or would they simply replace them with something else to hate, to avoid facing what they really hate—themselves and God?

The point is: that which we hate is in us. Jesus taught that when he said: "Love your enemies," and "Let the one without sin cast the first stone."

With these understandings of true justice in mind, we will examine cases which demonstrate situations in which legal action is necessary—and ones which demonstrate situations in which legal action only appears to be necessary.

Exxon's Rape of Alaska

The Exxon oil spill is a good example of incorrigible crime. After Exxon made untold millions pumping oil out of Alaska, its supertanker, the Exxon-Valdez, ran aground and spilled millions of gallons of oil in Alaska's Prince William Sound. The ecological damage was enormous, probably irreparable. Exxon was quick to blame the ship's captain. No doubt, he was immediately at fault. But do you wonder what was in his past driving and employment record? Do you believe this incident was the first inkling that Exxon had that this skipper was not reliable? Exxon certainly wanted everyone to believe that, but should we?

Now look deeper. Recall the steady trickle of news reports about how Exxon stalled the clean-up. Any sixth grade student could see Exxon's offers to clean up its mess were nowhere near adequate. To compound matters, Exxon had the daring to actually sue the state of Alaska for hindering Exxon's clean-up efforts. The grounds for the suit? Alaska would not allow Exxon to use potentially unsafe chemicals to clean up the oil spill. Be sure of one thing: Exxon will try to get out of this sticky situation as lightly as possible. It has no remorse other than the fact that it got caught. It will probably take many court battles to bring Exxon to task.

The Boeing Experiment

A CBS *60 Minutes* segment concerned a man who had contracted leukemia. He claimed he contracted the disease after being exposed to electromagnetic pulses (EMP's), which were emitted at his place of work. He worked for a Boeing plant in Montana. The lawsuit he filed alleged Boeing had known of the EMP problem for about twenty years and had been advised that its employees experienced a high rate of leukemia relative to what would normally be expected in a work force of the size employed at Boeing's plant. The suit further alleged Boeing conducted covert studies to determine the effect of EMP's on its employees, without advising the employees that they were being used as test subjects or of the abnormal rate of leukemia among Boeing employees. Of course, Boeing denied the charges, and the jury has yet to decide the case.

Suppose the allegations in this man's complaint are true. How would you feel if you were this man? Would you want to mediate this case with a company which denied any wrong doing in a case such as this? Look at it another way. How would you react if you were on the jury deciding this case?

If this man is correct in his allegations, and the evidence presented on *60 Minutes* seemed to strongly lean that way, then something certainly needs to be done about Boeing. Were it not for this lawyer, or another like him, this matter might never have been exposed. This smacks of what went on in Germany during World War II. Can you imagine the allies sitting down and mediating with Hitler or his henchmen?

Detroit Roulette

A Birmingham, Alabama law firm cracked the Ford Pinto rear-end explosion cases by somehow obtaining secret intra-company memoranda and test films revealing Pintos exploding in simulated rear-end crash tests. I am told the evidence presented at trial was substantially as follows: It was known by Ford that such explosions would occur in about twenty percent of such cases. Top Ford officials weighed the costs of recalling and remedying the dangerous defect against the costs of litigation and legal damages Ford might incur if no recall was made. The cost of the former was estimated to be about

$150,000,000 more than the cost of the latter. So the recall was not made.

Juries went wild when these facts were put into evidence. Are you going wild just reading about this? Ford and its management would have gotten away with it except for this law firm's tenacity about getting to the truth. As it was, they got off easy compared to what other murderers and arsonists get when they are convicted. How do you mediate with people who knowingly play roulette with other peoples lives and health?

Medical Gods

I once considered writing a book about what was really going on in the medical malpractice crisis, but discarded the idea after several unsuccessful attempts to pre-sell the book to a publisher. Before dropping the project, I did quite a bit of research into the matter. Although I did find many malpractice cases were nothing more than "stick-up jobs," many more were meritorious. These fell into four basic categories: (1) simple negligence by an otherwise good but self-righteous doctor, who did not want to pay for his mistake; (2) doctors who made mistakes and destroyed or altered their records to protect themselves; (3) incompetent doctors with previous reported violations and medical board investigations, making repetitive mistakes; and (4) doctors known by their medical boards to be alcoholics or drug addicts, making mistakes because of their addictive habits.

I discovered that in every state except perhaps Oregon, plaintiff lawyers were the only force regulating doctors. Pious doctors testified before the various state and national legislative tort reform committees that plaintiff lawyers were evil and brought frivolous lawsuits. That was about twenty percent true and about eighty percent false. The insurance companies, who insure doctors and well know of their competence or lack thereof — and drinking and drug habits, testified with the doctors (who pay the premiums) instead of with the plaintiff lawyers (who mostly told the truth). If it were not for plaintiff lawyers, doctors in most places would not have to answer to anyone for their misdeeds. How do you mediate with people who believe they are above the law?

These cases are but a small number of the many cases of social import in which a legal action is necessary to achieve true justice. Take a moment to think of other such cases. Perhaps the following suggestions will help you in this process: a President breaks various laws, then destroys the evidence and lies to the public and to congress about what he has done; a marine colonel lies to Congress and never admits guilt; a Speaker of the House of Representatives violates a variety of ethical rules he is charged with enforcing, and never once admits wrong-doing; a nuclear plant in Pennsylvania nearly causes a major disaster, and no one admits that a mistake was made or that there was any danger; acid rain poisons Canadian and northeastern American waters and causes all manner of air-borne diseases, and no manufacturers admit they have anything to do with it; a man in California kills and maims many children in a school playground with a semi-automatic rifle, and the National Rifle Association comes out even more strongly in favor of such weapons. Now it's your turn.

Most likely, you were able to come up with many other examples of cases in which a legal action is (or was) necessary to achieve true justice. Now I have this question for you: Are you truly in a position to throw the first legal stone in the cases you came up with? Here are participatory exercises playing on the Exxon, Boeing, Ford, and medical malpractice examples that will help you answer this question.

Exxon Exercise

Assume that you live in Alaska and engage a lawyer to help you represent all Alaskans in a class action case against Exxon. Before you file suit, answer these questions:

Are you a polluter like Exxon, even in a small way? Do you litter? Do you use ozone-destroying products or toxic cleaning agents? Do you use weed killers and pesticides? Do you buy foods which are grown with environmentally destructive chemicals? Does your car meet EPA requirements? Given your relative sizes, do you cause the environment any less damage than Exxon? Face your own contribution to environmental pollution, before taking Exxon to court. Then you will have earned the right to do that. If you do not first get your own house in order, you are not honoring "the truth, the whole truth, and nothing but the truth." You are honoring the truth only to the extent that it justifies your anger toward Exxon, which disguises the same anger you feel toward yourself.

Boeing Exercise

You are an employee at this Boeing plant. You discover that you have leukemia. You engage a lawyer to sue Boeing. Before filing suit, answer these questions:

Do you expose yourself to dangerous EMP's, as Boeing did you? Do you use microwave ovens? Digital watches? Electric blankets? Sit close to your unshielded television or computer monitor? Get frequent X-Rays? Are you injuring yourself with

EMP's any less than is Boeing? Are you only using part of the truth to justify your lawsuit? Would the whole truth create doubt in the jurors minds as to the true cause of your leukemia?

Ford Exercise

You are injured when your Ford Pinto explodes in a rear-end accident at an intersection. You engage a lawyer to sue Ford. Before you file suit, answer the following questions:

Do you create automobile hazards, as did Ford? Do you use your automobile safely? Do you keep your automobile in good repair? Do you observe traffic laws? Do you drive after drinking or using narcotics? Do you allow people who should not drive use your car? Given your relative sizes, do you create any fewer automobile dangers than Ford? You are entitled to compensation in this case, but you should also commit to doing your part to keep dangerous automobiles off our roads and highways.

Medical Malpractice Exercise

You have been injured by a doctor who has negligently treated you. You engage a lawyer to sue the doctor. Before you file suit, answer these questions:

Are you also guilty of committing acts of medical malpractice on yourself or on others? Do you or your family overuse antibiotics? Do you or your family regularly eat fatty and sugary foods, drink alcohol, or use over the counter or prescription drugs? Do you exercise regularly? Do you deal with your life issues? You are entitled to compensation in this case, but you should also commit to doing your part to maintain your health.

Now take a few moments to reflect on the cases you

felt needed some form of legal action to achieve true justice. Do you have a different view of these cases now? If so, how is it different?

Cases of broad social significance such as those above require some form of legal action, even when we have not put our own house in order. While it is wise to attend to our own dirty laundry first, that is not an absolute condition to righting these types of obvious wrongs. However, there are cases more individual in nature, where an over-riding social concern is not a factor. In such cases, getting our own house in order before suing or prosecuting another wrongdoer is much more compelling. Many cases in this book have already shown this. Here are a few more which further demonstrate the point.

The Cuckolded Husband

Jack discovered that Carol, his wife of ten years, was having an affair. Jack was enraged and went to a divorce lawyer about getting a divorce and gaining custody of their two children. The lawyer told Jack getting a divorce would be no problem, but getting custody would be a big problem because the courts no longer gave much weight to adultery not committed in the presence of the children. Jack said to his lawyer, "I don't care, I just want that bitch to pay for what she has done to me!"

Imagine that you are Jack. Do you share his feelings towards Carol? Do his actions seem justified? Would you think differently if you knew that when Jack was twelve, his mother died and he has never forgiven her? Would you think differently if you also knew three years earlier Jack had an affair which lasted six months? These unresolved issues almost certainly fuel Jack's rage towards Carol.

If Jack would allow himself to see how Carol mirrors him, he might develop a different attitude towards her. Instead of revenge, he might seek healing. He might wish to share with her his own unresolved life issues, and she might do the same with him. They might heal together, instead of inflicting further damage on each other and on themselves.

The Self-Righteous Mother

Eve sought a divorce from Landon. Their son, Lanny, was angry about the family discord and break-up, and misbehaved to express his anger. He screamed at Eve, ignored her when she talked to him, and broke things she loved. This was also how Landon treated Eve in Lanny's presence, so Eve felt Lanny's behavior was influenced by his father. When confronted with this by a therapist whom Eve hired to help Lanny, Landon denied any responsibility. Instead, he blamed Eve for everything. Underneath this was the fact that Landon's parents unexpectedly divorced when he was fifteen, and he never forgave them. The therapist suggested something similar was behind Lanny's angry behavior, and Landon said, "It's not the same thing; I was fifteen when my parents divorced and Lanny is only six!" Landon stormed out of the therapist's office and refused to help pay for Lanny's therapy.

There was much denial on Landon's part. Eve felt Landon's time with his son should be limited, even denied. This would have been a mistake. At a spiritual level, Eve, Landon, and Lanny made an agreement to be a family together. They have lessons to learn from and to teach each other. To interfere with this agreement would thwart much of their spiritual work. Moreover, to deny Landon time with his son would enable Eve to avoid looking at herself and at her own denial.

The therapist learned from Eve that she often screamed at Lanny when he did not behave to suit her, just as her mother screamed at her when she did not behave to suit her mother. Eve, too, broke many of her mother's favorite things to get back at her. The therapist also noticed Eve's tendency to "space out" during their sessions together. The therapist asked Eve if she did this with Lanny or with others in Lanny's presence, and Eve reluctantly admitted this did occur quite frequently. So you see, Eve also modeled the very behavior she wants to blame on Landon.

If Eve would accept how Landon and Lanny mirror her and how much like her they are, then she might end her determined efforts to change them and turn her attention towards changing herself and healing her relationship with her parents and with God, whom they represent to her. If she would do that, she would develop compassion for Lanny and Landon. They would sense this, and positive changes could result. Instead of fighting for the rest of their lives, this family could heal and get on with really living.

The Indignant Right-To-Lifer

A friend of mine, Jenny, is a zealous right-to-lifer. She participates in anti-abortion marches and lie-ins at abortion clinics. She is loud and regularly gets into arguments with pro-choice people. At a recent lie-in she was beaten up by pro-choicers. She came to me complaining about what had happened to her. She wanted me to help her find a lawyer to sue the abortion clinic and the people who beat her up. I said getting beat up was the risk she ran for forcing her views onto other people.

"If people do not want children, then they should not get pregnant!" she exclaimed. I replied that I agreed because children born to people who do not want them often do not fare well in life. I also said I wondered how to determine when an embryo receives a soul, or what spiritual agreements the souls of children make with the souls of their parents? She turned livid and said, "That's the talk of the devil!"

Who is right? It's not an easy question to answer, and I will not try to decide the spiritual right or wrong of abortion here, for I believe only God can do that. However, there are some things Jenny might want to examine— things I learned from her during our time together— things she did not want to face.

She came from a dysfunctional family. Her father was an alcoholic and very critical of her. Her mother, instead of confronting her father's alcoholism, took refuge in her fundamentalistic church. She imparted to Jenny a deep belief that she was an evil sinner. No doubt Jenny felt at a deep level that her parents psychically "murdered" her, and she hates God for what her parents did. Anything that reminds her of murder, such as abortion, triggers her hatred toward her parents and God. There's more.

When Jenny was fourteen, a good friend got pregnant. Jenny helped her friend get an illegal abortion. There were complications and hospitalization was required. Jenny's friend got in a lot of trouble with her parents. Jenny's mother never forgave her for helping her friend get the abortion. Abortion triggers the pain Jenny feels as a result of this experience. And there's even more.

Jenny has two young children of her own. She complained to me about their behavior—about how much she resented their demands on her time. They, too, probably feel psychically "murdered" by her. Abortion unconsciously reminds her of what she does to her children.

Jenny is not in the clear here. She needs to ponder deeply before proceeding with her crusade. That will be difficult for her, for it will reveal psychospiritual wounds and her own behavior are what fuel her anti-abortion crusade. She might also ponder this: the factors fueling her pro-life stance might just as easily have caused her to take a pro-choice position on abortion. For example, the abuse she experienced as a child could just as likely have caused her to embrace an attitude that this is not a safe world for children—that abortion is preferred to birthing children who are likely to be abused by their parents; her teenage experience with abortion might have caused her to develop the attitude that abortion should be legalized and thus destigmatized; her inadequacies as a mother might have caused her to form the unconscious attitude that abortion is preferred to being a mother.

If Jenny would allow herself to see how she could just as easily have developed pro-choice attitudes, she would find herself in the shaky zone and might then develop a more peaceful attitude towards those who favor abortion. If Jenny's pro-choice opponents would allow themselves to see Jenny as their reflection, then they might experience similar healing. Instead of fighting, they could all sit down and work out a solution which works for everyone. Or they might abandon their crusades altogether, turn their attention towards healing what really bothers them, and let Spirit do the teaching of others.

The last three cases demonstrate situations in which

people focused on another's error to avoid their own. This is a common theme in my clients' cases—so common, in fact, that I have yet to see one in which this was not happening. I would be quite surprised to find a case where the person who felt wronged did not have important unfinished business to attend to, before proceeding against the wrongdoer.

Of course, there are individual cases where it is appropriate to stand up against the Exxons, Boeings and Fords in our personal lives. Let's look at those types of cases.

The Beleaguered Husband

Ralph's wife, Julie, tried to take him in a divorce. She hired a woman lawyer, known in legal circles for her dislike of men. Julie wanted three-fourths of Ralph's $35,000 annual salary, sole custody of their son and daughter, the right to move with them to another state without his permission, for him to pay her college tuition, and for him to pay their children's private schooling. She also wanted control over their children's religious upbringing. This was the theme in their marriage, as well. No matter what Ralph did to please Julie, it was never good enough. All Ralph wanted in his divorce was a fair shake, but there was no satisfying Julie, who only wanted revenge.

Ralph's mother had been very much like Julie, making incessant demands on Ralph and his father, and as often occurs, Ralph married Julie, a woman like his mother. Julie hated her father and married Ralph, a weak man she could dominate and punish, and thus indirectly vent her rage towards her father. The divorce was, for her, the culmination of her vendetta against her father (and

153

God, whom her father symbolized), and Ralph caught the brunt of that vendetta. It did not take a Sherlock Holmes to figure out something similar had happened to Julie's angry lawyer when she was a child.

Knowing all of this was interesting to Ralph, but it did not help him in his case. He was, to use his words, "fighting mad," and I told him I didn't blame him. He wanted to hire what in divorce circles is called a "barracuda" lawyer (like Julie's)—one who is mean as can be, and whose bite is often lethal. I asked what did he think happened when two equally powerful barracudas got into a fight? He thought a minute, then said, "I suppose they chew each other up." And he was right, for that is the result in such cases—everybody gets chewed up. I then asked if he had not been chewed up enough by his mother and by Julie, barracudas in their own right? He laughed and said he had had quite enough of that, thank you!

I suggested he would not need a barracuda lawyer. The judge would not give Julie what she demanded. In fact, she would not get anywhere close to what she wanted. The courts have predictable guidelines in these types of cases, and Ralph would get a result around those guidelines. He could get that result without fighting. Rather than fighting, he could simply tell the judge about his assets and debts, his salary, and his desire to raise his children and share with them his religious beliefs, and then let the judge tell Julie (and her lawyer) how it would be.

And that is what Ralph did. It frightened him to hang tough without running or fighting, new behavior for him with the important women in his life. Yet he came out well for having done that. Julie and her lawyer angered the judge, and Ralph got more than a fair shake: Julie was ordered not to leave the state with the children; Ralph got liberal visitation; Julie got $700 per month in child support, and had to go to work; and each parent was allowed to teach their respective religious beliefs to their children.

This scenario is seen all too often in divorces, on both sides. It is not always the wife and her lawyer who act unreasonably. Just as often, the husband wants to starve out the wife and run off with the children. Most lawyers, even the barracudas, tell their clients they cannot get away with this sort of behavior, but that often has little effect. Why? Because the fuel is hatred. If revenge is the motive, then you have to stand up for yourself. The trick is doing it, as Ralph did, without counterattacking. If you counterattack, you will get back what you put out.

Had Ralph counterattacked, the case would have escalated into the typical blood-bath often seen in such cases: the children ripped apart and the scars lasting for life. Ralph, Julie, and their children might have gotten sick. Ralph spared his children and himself by refusing to attack Julie, and began the healing of his relationship with women. As to Julie, she hates men (and probably God) more than ever. Most likely she will find another man like Ralph to punish, or one who will treat her even worse than her father did. Equally likely, she will take out her hatred of men on her son. She will relate to men in these self-destructive ways until she turns inward and looks at what in her makes her hate men. Here's another case.

The Jilted Partner

Anita and Karen were partners in an advertising business. They enjoyed a good reputation, and made a comfortable living. Anita got divorced, and remarried. Soon she began acting very differently towards Karen. Behind the new behavior was Anita's new husband, who felt she was more valuable to the business than Karen. Anita made demands for more of the profits and the more prestigious clients. Karen felt this was wrong and said so. Anita became indignant and said, "You will hear from my lawyer," which Karen did very soon afterwards. A letter came from the lawyer containing many outrageous demands.

Fortunately for Karen, a buy-sell agreement had been drawn up many years earlier to guard against this sort of problem. She sent a copy of the agreement to Anita's lawyer, who did not know of it. He acted as if it was irrelevant, and continued making unreasonable demands on Karen. Karen stood her ground, and Anita left and began her own business. She called on several of their better accounts, in an effort to win them away from Karen.

The buy-sell agreement had a provision saying, in the event of a break-up of the business, the accounts would be divided by drawing lots, the first choice to be determined by a coin toss. The winner would get the first choice, the loser the next two choices, the winner the fourth choice, and every other choice thereafter. It also provided either Karen or Anita could ask a court to enforce the agreement by "specific performance." Karen called Anita and her lawyer about this, and was rebuffed. So she hired a lawyer who got a court injunction enforcing the agreement. Anita and her lawyer provoked the judge, who ordered Anita to pay Karen's legal expenses because she (Anita) had caused a needless lawsuit.

The result in this case seems just to me. Does it to you? Karen acted with integrity. She never attacked. She only asked for her just due. The judge gave it to her, and he gave Anita her just due, too.

Exercise

Take a moment to reflect on the material in this chapter. Notice what you are experiencing after having read it. Do you view the subjects of truth and justice any differently than you did before reading this chapter? If so, how do you view them differently? If you are a lawyer, do you now have a better understanding of how truth and justice are subverted in legal proceedings which encourage clients to focus on the mistakes of others and revenge? If so, what is it like for you to realize this? What, if anything, are you going to do about it?

There are legal cases in which a wrong has to be righted regardless of whether or not we have put our own house in order, and there are cases in which we right the wrong of another to avoid putting our own house in order. In both cases, we have important unfinished business to address. Once we get our own house in order, we are in a better position to dispense true justice to others. This is the truth, the whole truth, and nothing but the truth.

Chapter Seven

Lawyers As Saints

This chapter is primarily for lawyers. If you read my previous book, *Kill All the Lawyers?*, then you know I do not engage in unbridled lawyer-bashing. So if you are not a lawyer, and hope to see me pummel the lawyers in this chapter, you will be disappointed. I poke at them a little, but I do not bash them. There has been enough bashing in this country. It's time to explore new ways to practice law, and that is what I invite lawyers (and their clients) to do in this chapter. I begin by saying a little about the legal profession, its present functions, and its major weaknesses. Then I make several suggestions about how the Bar can change into something truly wonderful.

About ninety percent of the lawyers in the world live and work in the United States. A March 1989 letter to the editor in *The Wall Street Journal* revealed law graduates in the U.S. outnumber engineering graduates ten to one, while the reverse is true in Japan. Lawyers penetrate every fiber of our individual and collective being. People love to hate you, and quote out of context various sayings by famous people such as William Shakespeare ("The first thing we do, let's kill all the lawyers.") to prove how bad they believe you are. I wonder, though, what

American's lives would be like without you? Who would they gripe about, if they did not have you to throw stones at? Who would they ask to prosecute their grudges against their neighbors, if they did not have you around?

Having once been a practicing lawyer, I know all too well that people view lawyers as snakes, wolves, crocodiles, sharks, barracudas, piranhas, rats, and vultures, to name some of the animals which they are affectionately compared to in jokes about lawyers. It is interesting, is it not, that when they hire you, most of your critics expect you to act like those same animals towards their legal adversaries? Don't you think Americans should be more careful about calling you names or telling mean jokes about you, since they curse their own creation when they do so? Do they avoid looking at the predator and scavenger in themselves which you obligingly reflect back to them? Don't you think, if Americans were *really* tired of seeing you operate like predators and scavengers, they would quit feeding you?

Of course, there are many helpful things lawyers do— things which many people seem to overlook. You help clients arrange and wind down their affairs on earth, by writing contracts and wills. You help them adopt children, go into business, collect debts owed to them by others, and get them and their children out of jail—or keep them from going there. If a client is injured in an accident caused by someone else and that person—or the insurer—will not pay a reasonable and just amount to compensate for the injuries and economic loss, then you help recover what is reasonably due.

There are few shows more interesting than a good fight among the heirs of a person who died without a will— or with a homemade one, disputing business partners trying to divide up—or make off with—the assets of a business for which there is no buy-sell agreement, the buyer and seller of a home fighting over the terms of a homemade real estate sales contract, or neighbors arguing over a common boundary line which was never surveyed. Lawyers can easily prevent these problems. Without you, people would settle such disputes by fist fights, duels, and vigilante action.

There is an additional and very important function performed by lawyers: you protect Americans from big-time wrong-doing, such as the illegal schemes of Richard Nixon and Ronald Reagan and their cronies; the manufacture of defective consumer products, such as Pinto automobiles and Dalkon Shield contraceptives; the manufacture of toxic substances, such as asbestos, dioxin, agent orange, nuclear and other toxic wastes; the distribution of chemicals which pollute the air, destroy the ozone layer in the atmosphere, cause acid rain, and damage our waters; the practice of wide-spread age, race, sex, and age discrimination; and medical malpractice, unchecked by state medical boards.

What other wrong-doing which would go unchecked but for lawyers comes to mind? One that might trouble most lawyers is unethical lawyers unregulated by the Bar—lawyers who steal from their clients, charge for services not rendered, breach clients' confidences, take in cases and do nothing about them, promise results which cannot be achieved—or lawyers who are drunks, drug addicts, or otherwise incompetent. The Bar does not police such lawyers much better than medical boards police errant doctors. As a result, an increasing number of malpractice cases are being filed against lawyers. As usual, the trend began in California, but it is spreading.

A friend of mine is on a Bar committee set up to investigate the use of drugs by lawyers. He told me of various clandestine efforts to educate lawyers about drug rehabilitation programs. I asked if his committee had as one of its goals educating the public about which lawyers abused drugs—or alcohol? "No," he answered, looking surprised. I then asked if the purpose of the committee was to protect lawyers from themselves, or to protect the legal consumer from incompetent lawyers? "I guess no one ever thought about it that way," he said.

This example demonstrates the self-protective buddy system lawyers (and doctors, too) enjoy. Although I think lawyers police their own better than do doctors, lawyers could do more. Filing a complaint against a lawyer and expecting a disciplinary committee composed of his lawyer friends to give the client a fair shake is like the farmer putting the fox in his hen house to protect his chickens from the other foxes. If lawyers really want respect, they should get the fox out of the legal hen house.

They could do that by having lay people sit on legal disciplinary committees. The lay committees would use lawyers in an advisory capacity. Legal ethics and related cases are often complex and confusing. Legal expertise is needed in many such cases. Lawyers routinely use experts as advisers and witnesses. For example, in medical malpractice cases, a doctor might be suspected of malpractice, but only another doctor is legally qualified to testify as an expert at trial that malpractice has been committed. Similarly, lay disciplinary committees could use lawyers to advise and testify in proceedings against lawyers.

Plaintiff lawyers have accurately pointed out in legislative hearings that a big reason for the medical malpractice crisis is the fact that medical review boards are made up of doctors who protect incompetent and dishonest doctors. Lawyers would protest if juries in medical malpractice cases consisted of doctors, or if juries in product liability cases were made up of employees of the companies which manufactured the defective products. So lawyers should understand why the public is skeptical of complaints against lawyers being heard and decided by lawyers.

In order for lawyers to feel comfortable with this sort of arrangement, they have to know it will not be used punitively against them. Lawyers who go astray are no different from anyone else who goes astray. Many lawyers who misbehave are afraid of being disbarred if they "come clean" and go for help. So they have a negative incentive to seek help. A safe harbor needs to be provided for wayward lawyers. They should know they will receive therapeutic treatment if they turn themselves in—that they will be helped with their problems so they can return to being lawyers. This may require periods of suspension and restitution to clients in appropriate cases. However, the focus will be on healing, not revenge. Errant lawyers who do not turn themselves in will face the more traditional forms of discipline.

An attempt to impose these changes could be made from without by zealous reformers, but if a legislative attempt in this direction were to be taken without the Bar's cooperation, legislative lawyers, who control most state legislatures, would probably defeat it. If the Bar takes the lead and imposes these changes on itself, this would be an example few could ignore. Perhaps then doctors would be encouraged to adopt a similar manner of dealing with wayward doctors, which then would inspire other business interests to implement similar practices of policing their own. Lawyers could be heroes.

If the Bar does not take the policing and healing of its wayward members seriously, then I predict it will not be long before legal malpractice suits will become as popular as medical malpractice suits. I wonder if lawyers will then play the innocent victim by asking their legislative lawyer friends for protective legislation, the very legislation they correctly oppose when doctors and other self-righteous special interest groups apply it?

There are other ways lawyers, as individuals, can improve the legal profession. They can do it by providing the following legal services for a reasonable fee to the legal consumer:

1. In cases where a traditional lawyer is needed to handle a legal matter in an area in which they do not specialize, refer clients to one or more lawyers known to be *competent* specialists in the area of law involved. Traditional lawyer referral services do not screen lawyers for competence. For example, a lawyer with no experience in handling divorces, incorporations, or lawsuits can enroll in a traditional lawyer referral service and offer himself as being qualified to handle such cases. This occurs quite frequently.

2. Represent clients in their dealings with specialists by negotiating the specialist's fee, monitoring the specialist's work, acting as a liaison between the client and the specialist, helping the client with any problems which may arise with the specialist. In no case will the liaison lawyer take back or expect to receive a forwarding

or referral fee from the specialist, as that will result in a conflict of interest between the two lawyers and the client.

3. Offer second, blind legal opinions. Presently, few lawyers will second-guess another lawyer, especially without the other lawyer's permission or knowledge. This places clients in the position of having to ask for a second opinion and angering their present lawyer, a risk not many clients are willing to assume.

4. Mediate fee and other disputes between clients and their lawyers.

5. Evaluate client complaints against other lawyers, with a view towards recommending no action, initiating a grievance proceeding, or filing a malpractice suit. If a grievance proceeding is indicated, advise the client as to how to prosecute it through the disciplinary committee. If a malpractice action is indicated, refer the client to a lawyer who can properly represent the client in such a case. (Lawyers know who the legal malpractice lawyers are.) If none is available, then prosecute the case for the client. If the recommendation to the client is to make a grievance complaint or file a malpractice suit, assist the client in discharging the old lawyer and obtaining a new one.

Lawyers who provide these services will cause quite a ripple in the legal pond. They will be actively sought out as guests on local radio and television public interest programs. Newspaper reporters will interview them. Such publicity, which will be free of charge, will place them in the public eye and bring them clients. Traditional lawyers might not appreciate such legal services, and any lawyers willing to take such a departure from the regular way of practicing law will need to have fairly thick skin and a deep interest in providing a real service to humanity.

I wish to offer a caution to any lawyers who like these ideas about individually policing the Bar. Please review Chapter 3 about crusades and rescuing. Are you interested in policing your profession as Abraham Lincoln, Gandhi, or Ralph Nader would police it, or are you all charged up to save the world from lawyers? Be careful here, or your crusade will boomerang on you. Those interviews might go to your head, and cause you to think you are the "legal messiah." Don't forget: you need healing, too, and the more anxious you are to fix your brothers, the larger is the plank in your eye.

Another matter the Bar needs to address is punitive (exemplary) damages. Punitive damages are awarded in addition to compensatory damages in lawsuits to punish a defendant for doing something really bad and to warn similarly-inclined people that society does not tolerate such behavior. Punitive damages are often recoverable in cases such as the ones described in Chapter 6 involving Exxon, Boeing, Ford, and physicians who alter or destroy records, or who commit malpractice because they are alcoholics or drug addicts.

Punitive damages are also recoverable in other cases. For example, a reckless or drunk driver who injures another should pay compensatory damages: medical and rehabilitation expenses, lost wages, and the value of pain and suffering. The driver should also pay a penalty—punitive damages—for acting terribly and injuring another. The *Pennzoil v. Texaco* case is another case which demonstrates these two types of damages. The jury determined that Pennzoil's actual damages were 3.3 billion dollars. The statute under which the suit was brought required the damages be tripled to 10 billion dollars as punishment. The damages over 3.3 billion were punitive damages.

Some states have either outlawed or curtailed punitive damages. This was done to limit jury verdicts and to discourage plaintiff lawyers and their greedy clients from bringing so many lawsuits. The allure of punitive damages encourages people and their lawyers to file weak, even spurious lawsuits which might not otherwise be filed. The allure of punitive damages also encourages people with victim attitudes (most people) to try to make up for every bad thing that has happened to them by winning a huge money verdict.

Outlawing punitive damages is likely to create more problems than it will solve because that takes the pressure off those who can cause the most damage to people: physicians, hospitals, pharmaceutical drug companies, automobile makers, insurance companies, and heavy industry—the same special interest groups which lobbied for the protective legislation outlawing punitive damages. These special interest groups are thinly regulated at best and unregulated at worst. For that reason, outlawing punitive damages is a mistake, for that allows the special interest groups to inflict intentional or reckless injury on others and the environment without any serious threat of reprisal. It also allows unethical and incompetent lawyers to do that, too.

Rather than outlaw punitive damages, I propose the Bar lobby for legislation permitting punitive damages with the stipulation that they be paid into the collective coffers, less a reasonable fee paid to the plaintiff lawyer (to be set by the court) for rendering a public service. These monies could then be paid over to organizations truly devoted to solving our legal ills, organizations such as the United Way, the National Committee for the Prevention of Child Abuse, Ralph Nader's Public Citizen, and Ted Turner's Better World Society.

———————————

Not too many years ago, lawyers held themselves out to be "attorneys and counselors at law." They spent more time counseling clients about avoiding lawsuits than they did representing clients in lawsuits. Today, the balance has shifted towards suing and away from counseling. Lawyers need to return to being counselors first, and litigators second.

Most lawyers know their clients' legal problems are often products of their way of living. They see their clients focus on the present injury and play the avenging victim, rather than look at their own responsibility. Lawyers know that launching a legal attack on the other side does not solve their clients' problems and usually makes their clients' lives worse. Many examples have been given in this book which speak to this theme and could serve as guidelines for lawyers to work towards helping their clients heal. Here is one more, framed as a hypothetical case. Assume you are the lawyer in this case (even if you aren't one).

The Paraplegic Child

Suppose Mr. and Mrs. Baker ask you to represent them after their five-year-old son, Johnnie, became permanently paraplegic in an accident. He rode his "Big Wheel" in the gutter in front of their home, a place forbidden to him. A car full of teenagers smoking marijuana came by, and just as the car neared Johnnie, he backed his Big Wheel into the street into the path of the car. Mrs. Baker watched the accident out her kitchen window, as she talked to her minister on the telephone. The Bakers tell you the driver's father is a wealthy businessman. His insurance carrier's adjustor has already called and begged them not to hire a lawyer before hearing what the insurance company is willing to pay.

This is a dream case for you—absolute liability, two deep pockets, horrible damages, drugs, and jury appeal. You might be able to retire on the fee you will make in this case. What do you do? Do you negotiate with the insurance adjuster? Do you file suit and initiate a case that may take years to be concluded? Do you send the Bakers to a lawyer who specializes in these types of cases and arrange to receive a large forwarding fee when the case is over several years later?

Or do you help the Bakers explore and heal the rage they feel towards Johnnie for disobeying them? The rage they feel towards themselves for not teaching Johnnie better? The rage they feel towards each other for not somehow preventing this from happening? The rage they feel towards God for letting this happen? Are you interested in knowing that Mr. and Mrs. Baker used marijuana when they were younger? That they drink? That Mr. Baker's father is an alcoholic? That Mrs. Baker's older sister was killed years earlier in an automobile accident involving a drunk driver? That Mrs. Baker has become a born-again Christian, and she and Mr. Baker do not get along because of that?

Do you see how Johnnie's injury pokes into the Bakers' old hurts, reminds them of themselves, and seems curiously related to the religious problem which symbolizes their difficulties with God? If you do not delve into these matters with the Bakers, you will trade money for healing. You will help the Bakers focus on the injuries to their son and how much money they will get, and they will probably never look at these more important matters.

They (and you) will be much richer financially, but much poorer emotionally and spiritually. Not only will you divert their attention from the big picture, you will set them up for more trouble later. Their lessons will be presented in some form or another in an increasingly loud fashion until they are heard and acted upon. The Bakers may end up getting divorced or become ill. Or something else awful will happen to wake them up.

Knowing this, you decide to help the Bakers understand their spiritual lessons, either by talking to them yourself, giving them this book to read, or by sending them to someone who has the skills to counsel with them over such matters. They agree to this. They discover the enormity of their case—that it is a major intersection in their lives— that many of their old hurts are tied up in it. They see how similar they are to the driver of the car and his friends—that their positions could easily be reversed. They connect the timing of the accident with their religious differences. They see all their old unresolved hatred towards other people and perhaps even towards God.

The Bakers are awed and shaken by these revelations. They are frightened to think what else might happen if they ignore what they have learned. They want to work on these other matters and resolve them. As to their case, they decide they only want fair compensation—to resolve it as peacefully and quickly as possible. They say they are ready to proceed with their case on that basis.

What do you do now? Do you negotiate with the adjuster? Do you file suit? Do you refer the case to a specialist? Or do you suggest mediation? Mediation will not be easy for the Bakers, given the gravity of the case, but it is now a possibility. If they mediate, healing may occur, not only for them but also for the driver.

Unfortunately, face-to-face mediation between the parties does not usually happen in this type of case. The driver's insurance carrier, not the driver, will pay for the damages. This rules out mediation of the money aspects of the case between the Bakers and the driver. Even so, the Bakers and driver can mediate the emotional aspects with the help of a mediator. If the Bakers and the driver can work with a mediator, they will have an opportunity to openly and honestly confront their life-long fears of facing conflict. They will get to say to each other how they feel about what has happened. They will get to know each other. The driver may apologize, something he probably will not do if the case is not mediated. Much healing can occur.

A separate mediation could be arranged between the Bakers and the insurance carrier, with you advising them as to what is fair and reasonable. Of course, what is fair and reasonable is relative. If you plan to make a large percentage fee, taking one-third or better of the recovery, then the Baker's will be at a disadvantage in the mediation. If you will take five to ten percent of the recovery as your fee, or merely work on an hourly basis, that certainly improves their chances of successfully mediating with the insurance carrier.

So do you suggest mediation? You may lose a huge legal fee. The case of a life-time may go out the window. That is one way to look at it. Another way to look at it is, you are doing something wonderful for which you will be repaid many-fold. We cannot know how you will be repaid. That you will be repaid is a certainty. As you sow, you reap.

What about the other scenario? Instead of helping the Bakers look at their problems and use mediation, you take the traditional approach to their case and make the big fee. Under the legal doctrine of "aiding and abbetting," the driver of the getaway car in a bank robbery is guilty of bank robbery. If the people who go into the bank kill a guard, the driver is guilty of murder. This man-made law is derived from a higher law of aiding and abbetting. By helping the Bakers focus only on the traditional legal aspects of their case so that they (and you) can get rich, you are guilty (along with them) of spiritual error. At some point, this will come back to haunt you. We cannot know how it will come back to haunt you. That it will come back to haunt you is a virtual certainty. Again, as you sow, you reap.

You have to answer this question: To what extent am I my brother's keeper? You are not asked that question in law school. Rather, you are taught in law school that your duty to a client in a legal controversy is to win— period. You are taught little, if anything, about negotiation or mediation, and nothing about human psychology or the ways of God. My aim is to alert you to these things so you will not inadvertently damage your clients or yourselves any longer.

Here are the views of some of your fellow lawyers on this subject:

David is one of the better plaintiff lawyers in the country. He came up the hard way, working days as an insurance adjuster and going to night law school. He built his skills in the county district attorney's office as the chief prosecutor before going into private practice. He is so good that when he gets into a case the other side assumes that it is going to lose big and reacts accordingly. When I talked with David, he was upset about how other lawyers represented their clients.

"Hell, Sloan," he said, "I try to settle the case for a reasonable amount, but the defense lawyers are so paranoid they end up costing their client a ton. I almost always get a larger jury verdict than I would have taken in settlement. I have worked hard to soften my approach and develop win-win negotiating skills, but no one will negotiate with me. They would rather attack my character, which is what their clients want, and make huge defense fees, which they would not get in a settlement."

Robert is an excellent tax, securities, and business lawyer with a Harvard law degree and a New York University tax law degree. He, too, is concerned about how clients and their lawyers approach a case.

He said, "When I take in a case, both my client and the other side view each other as the devil. The last thing either wants is to trust the other. Often, the lawyer on the other side encourages this attitude because that will drag the case out and make him a larger fee. I view my main job as getting each side to see, understand and appreciate the other side's position, so the case can be settled in a somewhat friendly and expeditious fashion."

Christie is a domestic relations lawyer and legal mediator. She was a licensed psychological counselor before going to law school. After completing law school, she trained in legal mediation. She has an active law practice and can fight with the best of them when she has to. Christie's way of dealing with clients who come to her with a domestic relations problem is short and sweet. She asks them, "Do you want to heal, or do you want to fight?"

Harry once worked in a New York City law firm and now has an office practice in another state. He represents businesses, writes wills, draws up agreements, and acts as a legal mediator. He called after hearing of my work. I explained what I did with legal clients. He said he had tried to incorporate what I do into his law practice, but no one seemed interested in receiving those types of services. I suggested it would be difficult, as things now stand, to make a living practicing law as I do it—that few people would pay money to be told their legal problem was a spiritual lesson—unless all lawyers operated that way. He sighed in agreement.

Harry has stated the dilemma. The issue is money versus healing. Styled as a legal case, it would read, *Money v. Healing*. It's an old theme, one God knows well. Jesus spoke to this theme when he said it was more difficult for a rich man to get into heaven, than it was for a camel to pass through the eye of the needle. The choice is yours. You decide the outcome of this case in your life. If you go just for the money, you lose healing. If you go for healing, you win the pearl money cannot buy, and then the money, if you need it, will follow. Which approach will you take?

To resolve this dilemma will take time. You cannot reasonably be expected to change the way you practice law overnight. Nor can you be expected to work without being paid for your services. I suggest this: begin with one case, one involving a client who is open to working in the ways described in this book. Perhaps you interest the client in this approach by offering this book to read.

Or you tell a few stories out of it. Or you use your own way to do it.

After working this new way with one client, you offer it to a few other clients. After you show you are willing to work this new way, then clients who are also willing to work that way will just start showing up, as they did for me. People who need help are connected with those who can help them heal. And your clients will help you heal, too. For every one you lead to healing, you will receive healing in kind. As you sow, you reap.

There is another concern I wish to address here: It is: Do you need special credentials to do this work with your clients? No. The spiritual principles demonstrated in this book are not taught in college and university mental health courses or in medical school; they are not tested on mental health or medical licensing examinations; and they are not used by traditional mental health practitioners or physicians. Thus these spiritual principles in *actual practice* fall outside the realms of mental health and medicine, and thus are not a part of those disciplines. Furthermore, the spiritual teachings and practices in this book are found in the Old and New Testaments, as well as in most other ancient spiritual teachings, and, therefore, are protected under the United States Constitution from interference or control by the state and federal governments, or regulatory agencies thereof.

You do not need a ministerial degree to teach these principles. You do need a business license to operate a church, but you do not need a business license to teach spiritual principles and practices one-on-one to consenting adults. Nor do you need permission from the Bar to blend your spiritual beliefs and practices into the way you practice law. You already do that every day you go to work, as does every lawyer you know. You are the only authority you need permission from to do this work with clients. Your ego will say don't do it, but your soul may have different advice.

There is one last thing I believe lawyers could do. You could ponder the lessons your clients' cases bring to *you*. Sophisticated mental health practitioners know clients, especially difficult clients, mirror the practitioners' own unlearned life lessons. I have shared with you how my clients bring me my own unlearned lessons on a regular basis. This upsets me because I do not want to think I have more work to do. I would rather think I am "enlightened," or have been "saved"—that I have learned all my lessons. I see my reflection in most of my difficult clients' cases, and so do most practicing lawyers, whether they know it or not. Here are several situations in which lawyers saw their reflection in their clients' cases. The first is one of mine.

The Unstable Lawyer

Not long after I began to practice law, my first wife, Dianne, and I separated. It was a very trying time for me. I had enormous mood swings and drank too much. It is accurate to say I was hanging on by my finger nails. During this time, I represented a dentist, who is to this day the most memorable of my clients. He was manic-depressive, either on top of the world, acting like a god, or in the depths of depression, and suicidal. He had medication for this but would not take it. As a result, he was like a yo-yo: when he was up, he used speed and trafficked in prescription narcotics, which his profession made easy for him to do; when he was depressed, he was unable to function. I never was comfortable around him, often got angry at him, and was pleased when he quit using me as his lawyer. In retrospect, I see how closely we resembled each other at the time, and how much I could have learned about myself had I been awake as to how he mirrored me.

The Ex-lawyer

John, a volunteer alcohol and drug counselor, works as a nighttime librarian. I asked why he no longer practiced law? "I was a criminal lawyer," he said. "Most of my clients were involved in narcotics—buying, selling, stealing, transporting and using drugs. I was making a fortune. Every night, I hit the saloons and drank with my friends, many of whom were lawyers. My father drove my mother nuts, coming home drunk every night—or not coming home at all. My son ran around with people who reminded me of my clients. I tried to talk to him, and he asked me, 'What right do you have to tell me how to live? Look at you and grandpa!' I got mad as hell, but deep inside I knew he was right. I participated in an intervention with my father, and he went away to a rehabilitation center. Two years later, the bar association came down on me because I was getting sloppy with my clients' cases. I was charged with taking in fees from clients and then not preparing their cases. I was suspended and told to seek treatment for my drinking. My wife divorced me. I guess I was pretty much like my clients."

The Divorce Lawyer

Rhonda, a shrewd divorce lawyer, commands respect from her peers as well as the local judges. She represented

Nancy, who asked me to help her understand her divorce. Nancy had no money, and Rhonda agreed to represent her and ask the court to order her husband, a dentist, to pay her fee after the case was over. Nancy's husband was a habitual liar, and weaseled his way out of everything. He sabotaged his business so his income would drop. His motive was to starve out Nancy so their children would come live with him. That way, he hoped to avoid paying child support.

The court issued a preliminary child support order which Nancy's husband ignored. Rhonda scheduled a contempt hearing to enforce the order, and lost! Losing such hearings was a new experience for her. As was not getting paid, for she saw she would never collect a court-awarded fee from Nancy's slippery husband. Rhonda became irrational, and several times invited Nancy to fire her. The case was near trial, and Nancy could not afford (from either a money or a time stand-point) to hire another lawyer. She believed Rhonda was abandoning her, and indeed that was happening.

Nancy and I explored the aspect of money and abandonment in her life, and she saw the scenario in her case was the same scenario she experienced in her family. Her father controlled her with money, and her mother, a diagnosed mental case, never protected her. Now Nancy's husband controlled her with money, and her woman lawyer did not protect her and acted crazy (like her mother). Nancy saw she had to stand up to her husband and to Rhonda. Here I will speak only of how she coped with Rhonda because it is Rhonda's lessons we are searching for.

She wrote Rhonda a letter (keeping a copy for herself) outlining their agreement, her financial situation, the nearness of trial, and her jeopardy. Rhonda got the letter and "freaked out." Instead of being fired, she was told to do her duty. If she resigned, she would be guilty of malpractice. She was forced to stay in the case and fight for Nancy, even though she would not get paid for it. She was angry at Nancy, but could not afford to do anything about that. So she channeled her anger towards Nancy's husband. No doubt, this was one of Rhonda's worst experiences as a lawyer, which indicated how big a lesson it carried for her.

So what was Rhonda's lesson? Using Nancy as a mirror, it is likely Rhonda's father used money, rather than love, to reward and measure her. Thus she learned to value herself by money. Nancy's husband was not going to pay Rhonda. This gouged deeply into Rhonda's way of valuing herself and her relationship with her father (and probably with God), and caused her to want to get out of the case. This case presented these lessons to Rhonda. Whether or not she learned them, I cannot say.

The School System's Lawyer

I met Ted at a social function. I noticed Ted's wife was pretty bossy with him, and he seemed to go out of his way to keep her happy. Ted told me about his law practice, his main client being a school system. He said his contact within the school system was a woman named Cathy who was in charge of the school counselors. Ted said what a good job he thought Cathy did and how much he respected her. As chance would have it, Donna, a school counselor friend of mine, had worked under Cathy for several years. Donna had complained to me that Cathy was not respected by the school counselors. She always undermined their work.

Most of the problem students were abused by their

parents. Donna and her associates discovered this and began the process of helping these children heal. That required questioning the parents. The parents did not like this for obvious reasons, and leaned on the school principals, often threatening to sue. When this happened, Cathy told the counselors to back off. She did whatever she could to placate those parents. Often she let them transfer their children to other schools where there were different counselors. I shared this information with Ted, who said, "That's very interesting," and changed the subject.

On another occasion, I talked with Ted about how his school system dealt with the troubling issue of hyperactive children. He said hyperactivity was caused by a chemical imbalance and his schools promoted the use of the drug ritilan to manage hyperactivity. I asked if it were possible that hyperactive children were acting out what happened to them at home? He gave me a funny look, and changed the subject.

The evidence suggests Ted experienced abuse as a child at the hands of a woman and, as a result, now has difficulty with women and with being realistic about child abuse. His wife and Cathy mirror this to him.

The Defense Lawyer

Ralph is a first-rate insurance defense lawyer. He has more business than he can handle. I asked if he ever had a client who made him stop and think about how he defended cases for his insurance carriers? He grinned, then said, "One of our insureds, a man named Newell, was at fault in an automobile accident. The other side filed a large damage suit. Mr. Newell, came to me to talk about the case. He said he was at fault and did not really want the case tried. I told him we would not go to trial if we could help it. He asked what would cause the case to go to trial, and I said an unreasonable money demand from the plaintiff would cause the case to be tried.

"Mr. Newell gave me a serious look, and said: 'I want you to pay the plaintiff whatever damages I caused him. I didn't just buy this insurance to cover my ass. I also bought it to reimburse people for things I might do to hurt them. I do not expect you to shortchange these people because my insurance company is run by tightwads. You are my lawyer in this case, and if I feel that you are are not representing me, I will turn you in to the bar association. I will also tell the jury what you did, if the case is tried.' I can tell you I had never had a client say anything like that before. It really made me think about things. I settled his case, pronto."

I asked, "Well, after thinking about things, did you decide to change the way you defend insurance cases?" He just looked at me. He may be making too much money to change his ways. Like the camel, going through the eye of the needle may be difficult for him. It always is for people who value money more than their soul.

The Plaintiff Lawyer

Mike asked me to testify as an expert witness in a case he had filed for a client against a real estate broker. Mike said his builder-client had sold a house to a couple who insisted on many changes which Mike said his client made. Two days before the closing, the broker advised that the buyers were backing out of the deal and were buying another home (on which it was later learned the broker made a much larger commission). Mike thought the broker was guilty of double-dealing.

I knew the builder from when I practiced law. I knew he did not have an honest bone in his body—that there was more to this case than met the eye. I questioned Mike closely, and he admitted that the buyers contended the builder had not done all he had agreed to do to prepare the house for sale. I said there might be some truth in the buyer's accusations because I had seen this builder make false promises to buyers in the past. Mike looked into it and learned there was substance to the buyer's accusations. He was forced to confront his client about this, and a nasty argument ensued. Mike settled the case for much less than he originally thought it was worth.

Mike and I met afterwards. I asked if he had had similar experiences with people setting him up as this builder had done. He said such was the case: his mother had done this to him repeatedly, and there had been many other times when he had been "hung out to dry by my friends and clients," as he put it. I asked how that felt, and he replied, "Terrible, like I have been trampled on." That is how it feels to be a rescuer, and the person you are trying to help turns on you.

Mike became very interested in learning more about the victim-rescuer loop in which he had been embroiled all his life and which this case presented to him once again. As a result, he found himself more aware of the victim-rescuer loop and less enmeshed in it. He was quite appreciative of my intervention, which was a radical departure from what he initially expected when he called me.

Gandhi was a lawyer. He never took a case without first peering into the meaning it had for him. He always swamied himself before representing a cause. And he never used the courts to attack or achieve revenge. He only used them to create change. Gandhi set a good example, one I invite all lawyers to follow.

Exercise

Reflect over the next few days on some of your most difficult cases or cases which seem to have a recurring theme. Notice the similarities between the problems facing your clients and those in your life As you do this exercise, you will see the truth that will make you free—if you are willing to act upon what you see.

Lawyers who are willing to take the lead in delving into the problems within the legal profession, will be heroes. Lawyers who help their clients see and work through the lessons embodied in their cases, will be healers (not only of themselves and their clients, but of society). Lawyers who are willing to see their reflection in their clients' cases and act upon what they see, will heal themselves. Lawyers who do all these things, will be saints. I wonder how that will affect lawyer jokes?

Chapter Eight

Healing Our Legal Reflection

The United States has a forty-eight percent divorce rate; more women and children are killed and injured in domestic violence each year than in automobile wrecks; drunk driving, drug crime, mushrooming violent crime (murder, rape, robberies, gangs), hatred and revenge (manifested as a tidal wave of lawsuits) clog and, in many instances, halt our system of justice; pervasive and indiscriminate sex (manifested as venereal disease, AIDS), teenage pregnancies (manifested as abortions), hopelessness and despair of our young people (manifested in illegal alcohol and drug usage, and suicide), racial hatred (manifesting in a resurgence of the KKK, Nazis, gangs) hold our country in a death grip.

Many would say to me for pointing these things out, "Love it (America), or leave it!" That is not the solution. That is DENIAL. The evidence proves beyond any doubt (a tougher standard of proof than "beyond a reasonable doubt") that what we are doing is not working—that major changes are needed. Our families have failed us. Our educational system has failed us. Religion has failed us. The U.S. Government has failed us. And most of all, we have failed ourselves.

I propose we approach these problems in a different way—that we come out of our denial and look at the the root causes, so we will know what really needs to be done. We need to face the truth, otherwise we will never find solutions. Let's start with the biggest symptom— child abuse.

Children who grow up feeling good about themselves, happy about life, and connected to God within and without, do not turn to alcohol or narcotics, race or sex discrimination, crime, child and spouse abuse, obsession with suing people at the drop of a hat, weird dress, and suicide. School counselors, mental health practitioners, the clergy, and divorce lawyers know family trauma is pervasive in this country. The forty-eight percent divorce rate is only the tip of the iceberg. Perhaps another forty-eight percent of marriages are a living hell for the spouses, but they do not get divorced. Mental health professionals and people within organizations such as Alcoholics Anonymous, Narcotics Anonymous, and Al-Anon say over ninety-five percent of the families in this country are in some significant respect in trouble, leaving less than five percent of the families in the "healthy" category. It is not hard to connect these grim facts to the broad legal problems of our country.

My wife, Betty, a licensed social worker with ten years experience as a grade school counselor, told me that over the course of a four year period where she worked in a fairly typical middle class elementary school, she had been called upon to intervene in some capacity with an estimated eighty percent of the school population. She felt that approximately fifty percent of the children she worked with experienced ongoing emotional difficulty. She said these children were fairly typical of the students in other schools. I asked what she thought was behind this, and she said, "Lots of things; the main thing being the family situations."

Most parents believe they do a good job raising their children—that they do not abuse them. They think abuse means beating their children up or having sex with them. Of course that *is* abuse, and it seriously damages children, as many cases in this book demonstrate. Child abuse does not always take on a physical form. Sometimes it is much more subtle, but equally as damaging. It hurts children in ways few people understand or appreciate. It is like brainwashing. After it happens, children's lives are a mess, but they do not associate that mess with the abuse. Here are three cases which demonstrate how people experience legal difficulties without appreciating the connection between their legal woes and having been psychospiritually abused.

The Dutiful Son

Roger, a heavy-set man in his early thirties, has hypertension and depression. He copes by drinking beer, using cocaine, overeating, and chasing women. His first marriage ended in divorce when he was twenty-eight. His ex-wife moved to another state, taking their son with her. He seldom sees his son now. He came to me for advice about seeing his son more often. I asked him why he divorced. He said his wife and his mother could not get along. I asked him to tell me about his parents. Here is a synopsis of what he told me.

"I really love my parents," he said. "I would do anything

for them. Mom never seems to be very happy, and I enjoy doing things for her to cheer her up. I was always her 'good little boy.' Without my help, she would have had a very tough life. It was difficult for her when I moved out. I decided to live near-by, in case she needed me. Dad was different. He was a hard worker, but he never went to college and really wanted me to. I was a pretty good artist, but I knew Dad was right about college. I had a scholarship to a school of fine arts, but decided to go to junior college and study computer science so that I could get a good-paying job. I don't really like working with computers, but the pay is good."

Roger's life goes poorly. He sees no connection between his marital difficulties and being dominated by his mother. He sees no connection between his job unhappiness and having allowed his father to talk him out of studying fine art.

Most of our parents (like Roger's parents) want us to achieve what they have not achieved; want us to parent them, to make their lives work for them, and to adopt, and thus validate, their values which they themselves often question. We need to please our parents so they will love and accept us, so we usually do our best to do what they ask of us. When we do this, we quit being who we are and become someone else—the hardest job in the world. Our parents do this to us because their parents did this to them. Our parents know no other way to be parents, nor did *their* parents.

The God-Fearing Woman

Roslyn, a thin, wide-eyed, weary-looking woman has a history of paranoia and depression. She has been divorced twice, and her son, Terry, is into drugs and has been in and out of juvenile homes. Roslyn told me about her son.

"The minister at our church taught me about sin and the devil—that if I was not careful, the devil would end up owning me—that I should not associate with anyone who did not believe in Jesus. I tried, but could not make Terry understand this. Now the devil owns him."

Roslyn sees no connection between her paranoia and depression and her deep-seated fear of the devil, which her minister and family instilled in her. She sees no connection between her son's difficulties and what she and her minister did to teach her son that he was "evil."

Our parents (like Roslyn's parents) took us to churches where ministers told us we were evil and would probably go to hell. We heard statements such as, "You were born in sin," "God hates sinners," "The devil is lurking out there waiting to get you," and "You will go to hell if you do not believe in Jesus." We believed we were evil and acted in accordance with those beliefs. Our parents and ministers did this to us because *their* parents and ministers did this to them.

The Junkie

Henry, a high school drop out, is a junkie. He said he turned to drugs because he did not do well in school. I asked him to elaborate.

"I remember the first grade," he said. "My parents prepared me for it for over a year, telling me how much fun I would have, how much I would learn, how good I would do because I was so smart. I went to school full of hope. But it did not turn out the way Mom and Dad said it would. I just wasn't very smart. I wasn't good in reading or arithmetic. I was very good at building things, but we did not build things in school. My folks did everything they could to help me do better. They helped me with my homework. They even got me a tutor. But the best I ever did was make C's. The teachers said I had a learning disability. I could tell they did not like having me in their classes. I really let Mom and Dad and down. I knew I would never amount to anything after that."

Henry sees no connection between his parents' and teachers' investment in traditional education (at the expense of his natural talents) and his failure in school and in life.

Our parents (like Henry's parents) sent us to schools where, overnight, we found ourselves imprisoned and forbidden to move, talk, or laugh. We were ordered to memorize many things which did not prepare us for life and which bored most of us to death. We were ridiculed, humiliated, and threatened with failure by our teachers. We were measured by how well we could memorize, instead of by our more intrinsic qualities. We were treated in school very much like prison inmates, and many of us now act like people who have been in prison—helpless, angry, mean, and hurtful. Our parents and teachers did this to us because *their* parents and teachers did this to them.

The generational loop of psychospiritual child abuse, which the preceding material has explored, explains why so many of us have grown up believing we are unworthy, wrong, bad, and stupid—in other words, believing life is hopeless and we are victims. These are the conscious and unconscious messages we are given by the most important people in our lives, and which were given to them (and to their parents, all the way back up the line to Adam and Eve). It is not surprising that, deep inside, most of us do not think well of ourselves, or like our parents or other authority figures—or God for bringing such people into our lives.

If we were *unlucky*, some of the following misfortunes also befell us. We were born into a racial minority, and were discriminated against and felt rejected. Or we were born into poverty and felt deprived and empty. Or our parents divorced or did not get along, and we felt fragmented and somehow at fault. Or our parents were addicted to alcohol or narcotics, and nothing they said or did made much sense. Or our fathers were emotionally destroyed by serving in the unconscionable Viet Nam war, and we never fully experienced our fathers. If these things happened to us, we felt even more destroyed and resentful—even more hopeless and victimized, and even more angry at and disconnected from God.

Many people will say this description of how children are treated is too slanted—that it is not an accurate representation of what most children experience growing up—that I have been biased by my life experiences. This is a healthy response. It is important that we examine closely charges that we are spiritually destroying our children *en masse*, albeit unwittingly in most cases.

To clarify this examination, I offer the following exercise: please suspend your judgment on the extent of psychospiritual child abuse until you complete all four parts of this exercise. After finishing it, you will understand why Krishnamurti and *A Course In Miracles* (published by The Foundation for Inner Peace) describe love relationships as, *mutual* exploitation, and why Jesus said, "If any man comes to me without hating his father, mother, wife, children, brothers, sisters, yes and his own life too, he cannot be my disciple." I think Jesus used the word, hate, in the sense of breaking free or leaving behind, for reasons this exercise will reveal.

Swamicide Exercise—Part 1

This is a real hard-work exercise which will give you a chance to commit swamicide. Your ego will not like this exercise which is designed to reveal the degree of child abuse you have experienced—and have consciously or unconsciously passed on to your children. Most likely your ego will try to wriggle out of doing this exercise by the rules. Simply notice this if it happens, then follow the rules nevertheless. If you allow your ego to talk you into reading this exercise instead of doing it, you will not experience the truth about child abuse.

*You will need a friend (who is not your lover) to help you with this exercise. Nine questions are going to be asked by your friend. To each one, you are to answer **yes**, even though you will want to answer **no**. There is nothing else you will have to do, although the questions may indicate something else is to follow. After each question is asked, take a moment to notice what you feel knowing you will be answering **yes** to it. Then answer **yes**. Then notice what it is like for you to have answered **yes** to the question before receiving the next question. Here are the questions.*

1. Will you give me all your money?

2. Will you let me punch you in the nose?

3. *Will you let me have sex with you?*

4. *Will you learn what I tell you to learn?*

5. *Will you believe what I tell you to believe?*

6. *Will you always do what I ask you to do?*

7. *Will you always tell me what I want to hear?*

8. *Will you like me no matter how I treat you?*

9. *Will you live your life for me?*

What was this experience like for you? Did you see the absurdity but feel a familiarity at the same time?

One woman who did this exercise said it was a waste of time. I asked her why, and she replied, "No one ever asked me those questions, so they have no meaning for me." I said the questions were not to be taken literally— that it was the message behind them that was important. I asked, had people asked her similar questions or made similar demands? "Of course! Who hasn't had that happen?" she said indignantly. She then broke into deep sobs which lasted for several minutes. When she was calm, I asked what had happened to make her cry so deeply? "I was treated that way all of my life!" she sobbed, as the tears came again. She had come face-to-face with having been abused in her childhood.

Another woman in a large group of educators, to whom I was speaking on the issue of substance abuse prevention, simply refused to do the exercise. I asked why, and she said, "I feel you are trying to brainwash me like Jim Jones did all those people!" Another participant in the group said to her, "Miss, you are already brainwashed. Sloan is trying to unbrainwash you!" She never would do the exercise. It was too painful for her.

Most people feel badly to see how they let others run all over them—about how much abuse they have experienced. Please don't beat yourself up over this. Take a moment to reflect on what would have happened if you had answered *no* to these questions growing up? Would you would have risked rejection and abandonment, or even physical harm, by your parents and others important to you by saying *no*? So you chose to sacrifice yourself for their *conditional* love and acceptance. Unfortunately, in doing so, you separated yourself from who you really are.

Every time we answer *yes* to abuse, we dishonor and lose a part of ourselves, and separate further from God. Every time we answer *yes* to such abusive requests, we get angrier at others and at ourselves. Eventually, this anger turns into rage. If we keep saying *yes* to such questions, we get emotional indigestion. Rolaids, Tums, Malox, Asprin, and Bufferin help at first, but eventually more powerful remedies are needed: alcohol, prescription drugs, street drugs, and psychotherapy. Or we misdirect our rage by committing spouse and child abuse or other crimes, or by suing people. Or we litter and pollute the environment to repay society for how it has treated us. Or we dress "punk" or become "skinheads" to reflect the craziness we see everywhere around us and feel in ourselves. Or we become Nazis or Satan worshippers. Or we commit suicide, to complete the "murder" begun long ago.

Swamicide Exercise—Part 2

Now physically change positions with your friend, and you ask your friend the same questions. Your friend must also answer yes. Notice how your friend squirms before answering yes to these questions and committing swamicide. Also notice what you experience as you ask your friend these questions knowing you will get a yes answer to them. Now do the exercise.

What was it like for you this time? Many people who do this part of the exercise say they feel awful asking another these questions. Others feel angry at the other person for not saying *no*. When I ask them why, they say either they see themselves as the other person, or they realize they are guilty of asking such questions of others while expecting a *yes* answer. Did you have a similar experience? If so, what is it like for you to realize this? Do you feel stupid? Guilty? Ashamed? Please don't! Are these the same questions your parents and other important people taught you to expect *yes* answers to? Do you still ask people, including your children, these questions and expect *yes* answers to them?

Can we expect our children to say *no* to peers who want to involve them in drugs or crime, when we program them out of fear of rejection, and by our own neurotic models which they copy, to say *yes* to these kinds of questions? The transfer from saying *yes* to toxic demands to saying *yes* to toxic people, substances, and activities is natural and automatic. This problem cannot be resolved overnight. It will take time. It may take generations. As a beginning, we are going to have to give our children different messages, such as the ones listed below:

1. I want to buy *your* lunch.

2. I want to scratch *your* back.

3. Have sex with a person *you* choose to have sex with.

4. Learn what interests *you* and will help *you* enjoy and be successful in life.

5. Believe what *you* feel is true.

6. Do what serves *your* life purpose.

7. Always speak *your* truth.

8. Be with people who honor and respect *you*.

9. Live *your* own life.

These are messages your soul would like for you to hear and give to others. These are messages from God.

Swamicide Exercise—Part 3

To get an even better feel for how important it is for children to hear these last nine messages, ask your friend to say them to you one at a time, slowly. Take a moment between each statement to notice what you experience. Especially notice your feelings. They will tell you the truth. Then say the statements, slowly, to your friend. Notice what you experience as you speak, then share your experiences with each other.

If you did these exercises as suggested, then you are probably unhappy about what happened. That is how the truth often affects us. If you really want to get an eye-full of truth, do Part 4 of the exercise.

Swamicide Exercise—Part 4

Do each part of the exercise with your spouse or partner. Then with each of your children. Then with your parents. Then with anyone else you love. Go slowly. Do one person a week, or you may be emotionally overwhelmed. It will be less threatening for the others if they read you the first two sets of questions. If you read those questions to them, that may be too much for them. I leave this to your discretion. The last nine statements are less threatening. Even so, they will bring up powerful feelings, so be prepared for that. Much healing will come to you and those you love if you do this slowly, from your heart, without forcing or attacking.

———————————

Now let's look at some of the other big legal problems of our society. The street sales of illicit drugs in this country for 1986 was estimated at 140 billion dollars by the United States Department of Justice. A person at the National Institute on Drug Abuse said the Institute estimated there were 23,000,000 abusers of street drugs in the United States in 1987—that the actual number of users of street drugs was probably much higher. A Gallup poll taken in June and July of 1989 indicated that Americans view the drug problem as the most important problem facing our country. This is the first time in history Americans have ranked a social issue as the most important national concern. In September of 1989, the Bush administration unveiled a plan whereby much of the financial and enforcement responsibility for solving the drug problem was to be delegated to the states. The cost to the federal government was simply too great for it to shoulder any longer.

Our approach to dealing with this problem has been to declare war on the drug traffickers, both inside and outside of our country, and mounting a "Just say *no*" media blitz. We blame domestic drug rings, the Mafia, Latin American, Bahamian, Mid-Eastern, and Oriental drug kings for our drug problem. Are these people the reason Americans use drugs? Or are they simply suppliers of something Americans demand? Are we throwing our legal stones in the right direction? We would like to think so, but I do not think we are. And neither did Columbian Defense Minister General Oscar Botero, who to told a news conference in early September 1989, "The best aid the United States and other wealthy countries could give (Columbia) would be reducing drug use among their populations."

Most alcoholics and drug addicts use these substances to numb the pain of their childhood abuse. Without the alcohol and drugs, they only feel pain. When we ask children to say *no* to alcohol and other drugs, we ask them to say *yes* to pain. That is why so many people use drugs even though they know that they destroy themselves by doing so. It's difficult to take a long view when there is so much immediate pain.

That is also why it is so difficult for alcoholics and drug addicts to stay dry after they go through substance abuse programs and get these poisons out of their systems. That is why *ninety-five* percent of the people who come through the doors of Alcoholics Anonymous and Narcotics Anonymous return to their drug of choice according to insiders in those organizations. Working on the problem after it has occurred is not going to succeed very often. Drug abuse cannot be solved without first eliminating child abuse—and Viet Nam Wars.

The veterans of that war used drugs to endure the terrible pain they experienced over there, and they brought street drugs home and spread them throughout our country. Much of our street drug problem was seeded in that war, a war created by our political and military leaders who attacked the communist Satan to avoid facing the Satan at home, and by our business leaders who stood to profit by war. Now we must defend our country from the drug Satan we created through them. Under the law of agency, the employer is responsible for the wrongful acts of the employee committed in the line and scope of employment. The courts call that law, *respondeat superior*. There is a similar higher law. We are responsible for what our government, military, and businesses did, and we are reaping what we have sown through them. The law of cause and effect is exact. It never lets us get away with anything.

Another thing we need to do about drugs is get honest with ourselves about the true extent of drug addiction in our country. It is far more pervasive than we would like to believe. Here are the facts.

The National Institute on Alcohol Abuse and Alcoholism estimated there were 18,000,000 alcoholics in the United States in 1986. One family in four has an alcoholic parent in it. The Distilled Spirits Counsel of the United States reported the sales of all alcoholic beverages in this country in 1986 was $73.3 billion dollars. According to the U.S. Department of the Census, the per-capita consumption of alcoholic beverages in 1985 was 27.6 gallons, whereas the per-capita consumption of milk for that year was 27.1 gallons. The sales of cigarettes in 1987 were tabulated by Wheat First Securities Corporation (a securities house) at $33 billion dollars. The U.S. Department of the Census reported the combined per-capita consumption of coffee and tea in 1985 was 33.3 gallons and of sugar in 1987 was 164 pounds, almost half a pound a day. (This figure includes all caloric sweeteners such as syrup, honey, fruit sugar, etc., as well as processed sugar.) The annual sales figures for, and the number of individuals using prescription narcotics are quite large, but the Drug Enforcement Agency (DEA) and the National Institute on

Drug Abuse maintain these statistics are not reported by the pharmaceutical industry nor gathered by any government agency.

Until a few years ago, the number-one-selling prescription drug in the United States was the tranquilizer, Valium. Now the number one selling drug is Zantac followed in the number two slot by Tagamet. These are drugs for treating ulcers, a significant progression. Interestingly, a new Bristol-Myers tranquilizer, Buspar, was thought to be a major medical break-through. It is non-addictive, does not create a high, does not give alcohol or other drugs a "boost," and satisfies the major concerns physicians have about patients abusing tranquilizers. Buspar has not been well received because it only calms you down. You cannot get high from it.

Alcohol, prescription narcotics, nicotine, caffeine, and sugar are *legal* drugs in this country. Most people do not believe sugar is a drug. However, those who use it will learn how strong a drug it is if they cut it completely out of their diet. They will experience something similar to what people go through when they quit alcohol, nicotine, or caffeine, or stop using narcotics "cold turkey."

Are pregnant mothers turning their unborn children into drug addicts by taking legal and illegal drugs? Doctors and nurses who work in pediatric wards have many gruesome tales to tell about infants undergoing wrenching withdrawal after being born to mothers who use legal and illegal drugs. Are we turning our children into addicts by feeding them sugar and caffeine soft drinks from infancy? Are we pushing them to addiction with our own addictive model which they copy? A look at the advertising for sugar snacks, soft drinks, alcoholic beverages, cigarettes, coffee, and tea, and a peek in our pantries, refrigerators, and liquor and medicine cabinets will provide answers to these questions.

We condemn the drug kings while at the same time praise the chairmen of the board of the beer, wine, whiskey, tobacco, coffee, tea, sugary food, and beverage industries. President Bush and all but one Republican senator ardently supported John Tower to be our Secretary of Defense, although the F.B.I. had much information proving that Tower is an alcoholic and behaves unacceptably because of it. Our movie stars and professional athletes promote beer, wine, whiskey, tobacco, coffee and tea products, and others tell our children to say *no* to drugs.

I recently saw former President Reagan on television. He was at a party drinking a glass of beer. Why not just make a television ad in which he takes a sip, turns to the camera, smiles and says, "Just say *no* to drugs!" Or one in which pro-football stars standing at the bar in a saloon raise their Bud Lights and say, "Just say *no* to drugs!" Or one in which Clint Eastwood interrupts his conversation with a beautiful woman over a couple of whiskeys in a smoke-filled bar and says, "Make my day, say *no* to drugs!" Then would follow a printed disclaimer such as the following: *"Not included in this warning are alcoholic beverages, nicotine, caffeine, sugar, and prescription narcotics!"*

These scenarios would be pretty absurd. In essence, that is what happens in our media campaign against drugs. Perhaps it would be more effective if the commercials were reversed, and the children were told instead, "Be like me, say *yes* to drugs!" followed by a printed list of legal and illegal drugs. That would be a more honest approach, one children might think about and, in their rebelliousness, perhaps even disregard.

Are our children going to say *no* to drugs when they see this monumental deception going on? Are they are going to say *no* to "crack" when asked to do so in movie houses by movie stars, professional athletes, and other celebrities who use and even promote alcoholic beverages? Are they going to say *no* to marijuana because of warnings that it kills brain cells and affects sexual performance, when they see adults all around them killing far more brain cells and sexual responses with alcohol than marijuana will ever kill? Does it not appear that our so-called war on drugs is simply diverting our attention from the drug model we are providing?

The Gallup poll mentioned earlier did not include any of the so-called "legal" drugs in its survey, and for good reason: most of the people surveyed use those drugs. When I talked with my lawyer friend, who is on a legal ethics committee charged with the responsibility of examining and making proposals about the use of drugs by lawyers, I asked him what, if any, inclination the Bar had towards doing something about the alcohol problem which is far more rampant in the legal profession than the use of drugs. He said with a wry grin, "Very little, the lawyers on the committee all use alcohol."

This story reflects our denial of the drug addictive aspects of ourselves. We treat them as if they do not exist. That is like pretending the Viet Nam war was correct, the environment is not endangered, or nuclear weapons are not a threat to humanity. In order to heal the drug problem, we are going to have to get real about it. Otherwise, it will continue to haunt us. In fact, the more we deny its true extent, the more awful it is going to become. That is how denial works. The more we hide, the louder the messages we require to make us see.

The Prohibition experiment could teach us a lot about

this. The Prohibition laws transformed a good one-half of our adult citizens into criminals when they turned to bootlegged booze. Organized crime as we know it today was born as the result of efforts of well-intended-but-misguided religious groups who believed a reform law could eliminate a spiritual disease. Not long after the prohibition laws were enacted, we went into the Great Depression. After prohibition was lifted, we came out it and got into World War II. An interesting progression, yes?

Our government spent a fortune on law enforcement and lost an even bigger fortune in lost tax revenues to foreign manufacturers of alcoholic beverages and bootleggers. Billions of dollars in revenues that would have been received by American industry and paid to American employees and shareholders went to foreign manufacturers and underground figures. Billions of dollars were paid by Americans for expensive bootlegged booze, taking money away from other items of consumption. Prohibition was one of the most expensive mistakes we ever made. I think that we are making a similar mistake with drugs.

The federal government has no clue as to the cost of drug enforcement, for each city and county police department in the country is involved in it. I doubt our government really wants to know the dollar cost of enforcement. The cost is just too great to imagine. That is only part of it. If the Justice Department estimate of illicit drug sales being 140 billion dollars annually is anywhere close to being correct, then the drug market economy is nearly twice the size of the alcoholic beverage market economy. What about the lost tax revenues? What about the lost employee wages, business profits, and shareholder dividends? What about our balance of payments and foreign trade deficit? What about money spent on high-priced black-market drugs, which would cost only a fraction of the black market price in a free economy? What about money spent on these high-priced drugs that could be better spent on other things in our country? What about the cost in human resources?

Drug sales and usage in this country have increased despite our efforts. People will continue to buy and use these drugs for the reasons given earlier in this chapter. At this point, you might think I am going to advocate the legalization of street drugs. I admit there are attractive arguments being made along those lines. Certainly, legalization would give us a huge economic boost and put the drug traffickers out of business. The money hemorrhage and drug crime would disappear overnight. Our legal drug manufacturing companies would suddenly find themselves with rather hefty direct competition, quite a few employees in our law enforcement establishment would be out of work, and our polititical leaders would have to find another Satan "out there" to protect them—and us—from the mirror.

Countries such as Belgium legalized many street drugs, and have actually experienced a *decrease* in their use by removing the allure of the forbidden fruit. However, I do not think the Belgians faced the root problem. They simply legalized a symptom. This may be a step in the right direction, or it may be a step towards even greater denial. The jury is still out on that issue, for only time will tell if the Belgians are going to see and do something about the deeper issues, or whether they are going to be content with symptomatic relief.

We are never going to make any real headway with this problem until we do something about why so many people feel they cannot get along in life without drugs.

This is going to be a wrenching but necessary process for us to go though. We can choose to look in the mirror, or we can choose to bankrupt our country with our diversionary war on drugs. If we choose bankruptcy, will we then self-righteously blame organized crime, the drug lords, communism, and Satan for our plight? Will the drug lords of our "legal" drug companies then laugh all the way to the bank, as we numb our pain with even more of their intoxicating products?

We have also declared war on crime. According to the U.S. Bureau of the Census, there were about 13,200,000 violent and property crimes reported in this country for 1986, affecting thirty percent of our households. The U.S. Department of Justice reported violent crimes rose forty-three percent between 1977 and 1987. These figures do not include drunk driving, using or trafficking in drugs, racketeering, environmental, white collar, anti-trust, civil rights, and other serious crimes which would probably bring the total to dozens of serious crimes per year *per person* in the United States. Nor do these statistics include crimes like Exxon's oil spill in Alaska or the political crimes of Richard Nixon, Ronald Reagan and their cronies; or the crimes of the James Wrights in Congress.

It is interesting that the worst crime problem in our country is reported by the news media to be in our capitol, where crime is so bad President Bush considered calling in the National Guard and the Army to quell the criminals running amok there. Perhaps that is an appropriate action at one level. However, we might want to step back and ponder the directional arrows pointing at Washington, and the often-heard adage, "Birds of a feather flock together." Is it mere coincidence that our worst crime problem is centered around our nation's lawmakers. Do our lawmakers symbolize the lawlessness of our country? Are they drawn from a corrupt society, and will they change before we change? Are the common criminals in Washington doing us a big favor by bringing our attention to this fact?

In the summer of 1989, the Washington D.C. based Department Of Energy (DOE), charged with the responsibility of overseeing the production of nuclear products and the disposal of nuclear waste, was caught red-handed by the F.B.I. and the Environmental Protection Agency (EPA) in an apparent criminal conspiracy to conceal dangerous nuclear waste at the Rocky Flats nuclear weapons plant near Denver, and perhaps at several similar nuclear weapons plants around the country. These plants are operated by large, economically and politically powerful corporations under licenses from the federal government. After being caught, the DOE asked for 150 billion dollars to clean up the mess it allowed to be created. The money will come from taxpayers, not from the corporations which produced the waste. An unnamed EPA official was quoted by the newspapers as saying the DOE had had five years to build adequate treatment facilities at these plants, but instead spent that time arguing that its nuclear plants should not be covered by federal hazardous waste laws.

In the summer of 1989, several employees within the Food and Drug Administration (FDA) pleaded guilty to accepting pay-offs from large drug manufacturers seeking approval for new generic drugs. This was a continuation of corruption within the FDA, corruption which has been under criticism by Dr. Sidney Wolfe, head of the Public Citizen Health Research Group, a Washington-based public-interest group founded by Ralph Nader. Dr. Wolfe was quoted in the New York Times on August 14, 1989 as saying Dr. Frank E. Young, the FDA Commissioner, is "the worst commissioner I have ever seen." Dr. Wolfe added, "The sooner Dr. Young leaves or is driven out, the better it will be for public safety."

The November 6, 1989, issue of *The New Republic* carried a story about how our national government has known since 1980 that most of the chemicals needed to convert coca leaves into cocaine were made and supplied by major and politically powerful American chemical companies. Congress attempted to pass a bill with teeth in it that would severely curtail such sales, but the chemical manufacturing lobby cried so loudly that a toothless bill was passed, one that required notice to be given of sales to *new* accounts, but not to *old* ones. Bush administration spokespersons defended the legislation with the usual political double-talk, and then promoted escalating the already unsuccessful war on drugs. Later it came out that the bulk of shipments of these chemicals originated in Houston, Texas, President Bush's home state, and that the chemical companies making the shipments had pressured the government into not revealing their identities, fearing a consumer boycott of their products.

In September of 1989, the Department of Housing and Urban Development (HUD) auditors reported no improvement in the longstanding corruption and mismanagement in the foreclosure and disposition of HUD real-estate properties. In October of that year, further disclosures were made about how a housing rehabilitation program was milked for millions of dollars in excess rents and that subsidies apparently had been steered to developers who hired well-connected (to the U.S. Government) consultants. All told, the losses are estimated at 6 billion dollars, according to an Associated Press article of December 6, 1989.

That same article said the HUD scandal was small potatoes compared to some of the others being uncovered by Senator John Glenn and the Office of Management and Budget, including an estimated 56 billion dollars in lost Department of Defense property in the hands of contractors and a 58.8 billion dollar short-fall between Social Security receipts and social security payments reported to the IRS. The list of potential problem areas where money had fallen through bureaucratic cracks was 27 pages long!

Here are some other events which support the assertion that our government is our national crime model: Richard Nixon was pardoned; high government officials, such as House Speaker James Wright, were protected from criminal prosecution by political maneuvering and high-priced lawyers; Colonel Oliver North received a suspended sentence, and former President Reagan was protected from prosecution on grounds of "national security;" President Bush, a longstanding card-carrying member of the National Rifle Association, did not ban the sales of semi-automatic military rifles in this country; and Silverado Savings & Loan of Denver, of which President Bush's son, Neil, was a director, and Larry Mizel, a Republican Party fund raiser was an investor, was allowed to remain open long after federal regulators knew it was going down the tube. The cost to tax payers? Perhaps 1 billion dollars. The cost of the entire savings and loan debacle? I doubt we will ever really know.

What do common criminals think when they see these things happening? What do they think about the politically powerful Chairman of the Board of Exxon not serving time for what his company did to Alaska? What do they think about going to prison for selling drugs, when drunk drivers who injure people usually receive only fines, lose their driver's licenses, and do community service, and white collar criminals get off with probation, fines, and community service? What do they think when they see the CEO's of alcoholic beverage manufacturers owning mansions, vacation homes, and Mercedes Benzes? What messages are we sending to the common criminals about crime in this country?

The crime solution is similar to the drug solution. We have to quit raising damaged children, and have to provide a different role model that treats all crime pretty much the same. We have to get real, and that is going to hurt. Healing hurts when we have been in denial for so long, a fact any recovering alcoholic or drug addict can attest. The alternative to healing is more crime, just as the alternative to healing for an alcoholic or drug addict is more booze or more drugs. Are we hurting enough to be honest with ourselves, or are we going to keep running from our reflection?

At least one-third of our households were affected by lawsuits filed in 1986, according to the Center for State Courts and the U.S. Courts Administration. Many say, "It's all those greedy lawyers fault!" Most lawyers enjoy being well fed and do plenty to promote people filing lawsuits. Even so, who creates the injuries to people and property? Who takes the grievances to lawyers? Who makes the problems that judges and juries have to decide? Who raises the children who feel hungry, discriminated against, resentful and otherwise victimized? Who raises the children who grow up and get even by suing others, or try to make themselves whole by winning a big lawsuit? Who makes these children? Is it the lawyers? Is it the judges? Is it the juries? It is you and I, is it not? The following case demonstrates the point.

The Fifty Year-Old Lawsuit

Al, a real estate broker, was distraught about a lawsuit in which he was going to be called as a witness, and he told me how he got involved in the case. He said he brokered and made a commission on a real estate deal in which his friend, Tony, bought a piece of land from a ninety-four year-old man living in a nursing home. The elderly man told them the land was 1.1 acres in size. Tony decided to buy the property. He built a large home on it, then applied for a mortgage loan. The lender required a survey, which revealed the property was only .9 acre in size. Tony was enraged, hired a lawyer, and filed a million dollar lawsuit against the old man.

"I can't believe what Tony is doing! This is crazy!" Al shouted. "Why would anyone do anything like this?!! I'm considering ending my friendship with him!" I asked Al how long he had known Tony. "Over ten years. How could a guy I have known for so long do something like this to me!!!" I asked, did he really want to know? "Sure I do!" he shot back.

"Well, over the time that you have known Tony, have you known him to be a happy, easy-to-get-along-with person?" I asked.

"Well, not really."

"How long do you think he has been like this, Al?"

"Probably all of his life."

"How old is he?"

"Fifty or so."

"Well, this is a fifty or so year old lawsuit."

"Yeh, I guess it is," Al said with a sad look in his eyes.

"There's one other thing, Al."

"What's that?"

"Why didn't you tell Tony to require the seller to furnish a survey showing the acreage was 1.1 acres, if that was so important to him?"

"I don't know. I guess I should have done that, shouldn't I?" Al said dejectedly.

"Yes, you should have, and I think that Tony is really mad at you, but is not able to tell you that and is taking his anger out on this old man. What do you think?"

"Oh my God, I feel awful! Al exclaimed.

Unfortunately, Al did not feel badly enough to go to Tony and take responsibility for not protecting him. In this case are three of the main causes of lawsuits in this country: a lifetime of resentment; inability to directly express anger; and fear of taking responsibility for mistakes. The lawsuit solution is the same as the drug and crime solution. We must solve the core problem—damaged children.

Several people who previewed this book were troubled by this chapter. They agreed about the impact of child abuse, but, like stern fathers, felt strongly that we all must grow up and act like adults. As many parents say, "Shape up, or ship out!" Al, in the last case, had a perfect opportunity to grow up, but didn't. Instead, he acted as he had since he began to talk. Ninety-five percent of the people in this country are like Al. They need to grow up. They do not grow up because they are too damaged. They cannot say *yes* when they mean *yes*, and *no* when they mean *no*. They cannot express their feelings. They are terrified of being real or of taking responsibility for their actions.

For the most part, we approach problems remedially—after the fact. For example, religion focuses on "saving" people after they become sinners. Many Christians view children as wild beasts who must be tamed and brought to God. They forget Jesus said, "Except as a child, you cannot enter the Kingdom." Conventional medicine approaches dis-ease after the fact. Psychology tries to overcome the psychic damage previously done. Lawyers, judges, and law enforcement officials spend most of their time trying to correct or undo the messes other people have made. Remediation is not getting the job done, as the statistics quoted earlier in this chapter prove beyond any doubt.

We need to put much more focus on prevention. "An ounce of prevention *is* worth a pound of cure." Let's quit hurting our children. Let's quit sending them off to fight unconscionable wars. Let's love, nurture, and protect them instead. Let's raise children to feel and believe they are unique, valuable human beings—that it's right and just for them to be real—that it's sane, healthy, and safe to say *yes* when they mean *yes*, and *no* when they mean *no*—that it's insane, unhealthy, and dangerous to pretend they like being mistreated so we won't completely reject and abandon them. Then, they will become responsible adults, instead of breeding stock for more legal problems. Then they will like, instead of hate and fear, their parents and God.

Before ending this chapter, there is one more thing I wish to say: I believe our collective effort to cast the blame for our nation's broad legal problems outside ourselves— to avoid the mirror—evidences our nation's deep separation from God within and without. We can measure our return to God by the amount of responsibility we take for what *we* have created.

Exercise

Take a few moments to reflect on the material in this chapter. What are you feeling after reading it? Do you now view the broad legal ills of our country any differently? If so, how do you view them differently? What, if anything, are you going to do about it?

———————————

We cannot heal our broad legal problems by declaring contrived and arbitrary wars on them. They do not go away when we do that; rather, they get worse. That is what happens when we run away from ourselves and play the innocent, self-righteous victim. In order for us to heal our legal ills, we are going to have to view them as our reflection. That collective act of swamicide will put us in the shaky zone *en masse*, and scare us out of our wits. Unfortunately, there is no other way to do it. Fortunately, as soon as we do it, we will open to healing. If we do not alter our course, the ante will be upped until we respond—or break.

Closing Remarks

I wish to thank you for reading this book for I know it may not have been an easy one to read. Before you retire to deliberate, I wish to briefly review the more salient points.

There is far more to your legal problem than you can see. It is a major intersection in your life. (And if you are a lawyer, your client's legal problem probably reflects a major intersection in your life as well.) It is not an accident, whim of fate, Divine retribution, or all somebody else's fault. You consciously or unconsciously helped create your legal problem, and your spiritual lessons are mirrored by it. You can learn those lessons now, or you can wait until they are presented again. You cannot know how your lessons will next be packaged, but you can be certain they will come over and over again until you learn them.

First, look for the big picture—your relationship with God within and without, and do something about that. Then attend to your other lessons: remove the plank from your own eye before you attempt to take the splinter out of your legal reflection's eye. If you reverse the process, that blinds you to your lessons.

You may not be able to see your lessons on your own. This is to be expected, since you have avoided them all your life. Find a trusted friend who is honest with you—a person whose honesty has made you uncomfortable and angry in the past. Let that person help you see your lessons. Be open to "voices" which tell you to do things you don't want to do. Watch for dreams and uncanny coincidences which parallel and remind you of your legal problem. Gather the evidence which is everywhere around you, figure out your lessons, and act on them.

Once you see your lessons, you may want to stop the case. If so, apologize for your contribution to the problem and withdraw. Let Spirit teach your legal reflection. Then deal with your lessons and get on with your life, using your new wisdom to live it more fully.

If you feel you need to proceed with your case, first deal with your lessons. Then apologize for what you may have done to contribute to the problem, and propose mediation. If your proposal is accepted, invite your legal reflection to speak truthfully. Listen to what is said without interrupting. Imagine what your reflection must feel like. See how your reflection resembles you. You do mirror each other in some important way. Then tell your side. Share your feelings and concerns. Do not blame and attack, for you invite others to blame and attack you when you do that. Seek common interests, rather than differences. Find what you like about your reflection, so you can like yourself more.

If your reflection will not mediate, and you feel you must proceed to trial, do so with compassion. Be firm, but do not attack. State the the truth, the whole truth, and nothing but the truth, and let the judge or jury decide the outcome.

If you are a lawyer, you have an extra role to play. Not only do you need to heal yourself, you are in a unique position to bring your clients to healing. I invite you to view yourself as an officer of God as well as an officer of the Court.

"Render unto Caesar that which is Caesar's, and unto God that which is God's."

If you are concerned about the legal mess in our country, remember that what you do not like "out there" reflects something you do not like in yourself. If you want to change that reflecton, first change yourself and how you relate to others, especially to children.

That summarizes how you can take the high legal road. However, there is something else I wish to speak to in closing. It is how to teach the high legal road to others. When I first undertook to teach and advise, I made a bundle of mistakes. Out of those mistakes, I discovered seven important teaching principles. I am more effective with others (and save myself much grief) when I follow these principles. Here they are:

EXAMPLE. The best way to teach, always, is by example. If you use the high legal road, then others will follow your lead without your having to say or do anything.

EXPERIENCE. You cannot teach what you have not lived. If you attempt to teach others the high legal road (or any other road) before you travel it, you set yourself up for difficult lessons—lessons in arrogance, pride, and ignorance. As the Dervish teacher said to the upstart young Gurdjieff before he became a spiritual master, "Let God kill him who himself does not know and yet presumes to show others the way to the doors of His Kingdom." *Meetings With Remarkable Men*, G.I. Gurdjieff.

INVITATION. Offer healing only to those who ask for it. It is okay to suggest that you might know something helpful, but let the other person decide if he or she wants to hear what you have to say. Otherwise, you are likely to fall into the unhappy victim-rescuer loop described in Chapter 3.

GENTLENESS. Do not force anyone to accept what you have to say. Force creates resistance, which is used to protect from being further damaged by force. Force reinforces and deepens old hurts which were caused by force. Force violates the first rule of healing, as postulated by Hippocrates: "First, do no harm." As Jesus said, if people do not want to hear what you have to say, shake the dust off your shoes on their door-step and leave.

DETACHMENT. Your job, as teacher, is to share what you know on a take-it-or-leave-it basis. Let the person who has come to you for help make ALL decisions, even if you do not agree with the result. An exception is when you believe someone will attempt suicide or will injure or kill another person (or has already done so). In that case, make a report to the proper authorities. You should disclose this exception (preferably in writing) to everyone you work with, before you begin to work together. Otherwise, you put yourself in the position of betraying a trust.

INTEGRITY. The more troubled you are by a person who has asked for your help in a case, the more likely you see something in that person or the case that you have not resolved in yourself. When you notice personal discomfort, take a timeout. Discover what it is in you that this person or the case has triggered. If you cannot put your discomfort aside, withdraw. Otherwise, you are likely to make matters worse for both of you. Explain why you must withdraw—that it is something in you, not something in the other person, that requires you to withdraw. Even if you feel you can put your discomfort aside, you should share it with the person and let him or her decide whether or not to continue working with you.

RESTRAINT. Teach with restraint as embodied in *Tao 58* of the *I Ching*.

Therefore the sage is sharp but not cutting
Pointed but not piercing
Straightforward but not unrestrained
Brilliant but not blinding.

If you use your healing sword indiscriminately or to show off, you will attract to you other sword-swingers who will teach you about restraint.

I tried to follow these principles in writing this book. No doubt I fell away from them in places, and for that I will attract more lessons which will bring me further healing if I am alert, and make me suffer if I am not. Please overlook my human failings during your deliberations. Listen to the arguments of your ego, but heed the wisdom of your soul. Make your decision, the decision you know in your heart to be correct. Then take whatever action is required.

This book is the best way I know to share what I have been taught and what my clients and I are discovering together. My clients and other teachers join me in inviting you to take the high legal road. I wish you peace.

Appendix A

Preliminary Agreement Between Pennzoil and Texaco Regarding Getty Oil Company

1. Both sides agree that Getty has hidden value greater than what either side has agreed to pay for it. Without this hidden value, neither side would have tried to purchase Getty.

2. Both sides genuinely feel they are legally entitled to Getty.

3. Both sides are prepared to litigate their claims to Getty.

4. Only one side can win the litigation.

5. The outcome of litigation is in question.

6. If Pennzoil loses the litigation, it will lose the hidden value in Getty.

7. If Texaco loses the litigation, it will have to pay Pennzoil the hidden value in Getty, which will be trebled under the anti-trust laws.

8. The costs of litigation will be enormous for Texaco and Pennzoil.

9. Both company's public stock and bonds will be very much affected during and after the litigation. The loser's stock and bonds will almost certainly take a beating. None of this is desirable.

10. The litigation will divert the time and energies of each company's management away from normal operations. This is not desirable.

11. This dispute would have been avoided had Pennzoil put its agreement with Getty into writing.

12. This dispute would have been avoided had Texaco waited for Pennzoil and Getty to conclude their negotiations before making an offer to Getty.

13. An equitable division of the hidden value in Getty would avoid the economic hazards and expenses of litigation and leave both Pennzoil and Texaco in substantially improved financial positions. This would be positively reflected in the market price of their stock and debentures, as well as in their credit ratings.

14. An equitable division of the hidden value in Getty would allow management to get on with normal business matters, and would avoid emotionally damaging the employees and stockholders of both companies.

15. Both sides agree that Getty has played Pennzoil and Texaco off against each other. Therefore, Getty should contribute towards any settlement that is reached between Pennzoil and Texaco, and Pennzoil and Texaco will stage a "play" for Getty's benefit to produce that result. If Getty cannot be persuaded to contribute to a three-way settle-

ment, then Pennzoil and Texaco will meet again with the mediator and continue to work on resolving this matter in a mutually advantageous fashion.

_____

Mr. Penn, for Pennzoil

_____

Mr. Tex, for Texaco

Appendix B

Preliminary Agreement
Between Janet and Peter

1. The marriage cannot be saved, and a divorce is imminent.

2. The parents are having a hard time adjusting, and this is normal. The parents agree that it is best not to fight at this time.

3. It is important that the children feel loved by, and continue their relationship with, both parents.

4. It is not good to fight in front of the children. Future arguments will be held away from them.

5. Each parent acknowledges the other as a good and loving parent.

6. The parents agree to speak well of each other in front of the children.

7. Living apart costs more than living together. Therefore, everyone will eventually have to make do with less money.

8. Peter agrees not to abandon Janet and the children financially.

9. Janet agrees not to spend money on things that are not needed.

10. Janet wishes to be financially self-sufficient, and Peter also wishes this.

11. Peter is willing to give Janet a reasonable time to attain financial self-sufficiency, and will provide extra financial support.

12. Peter agrees for now not to have his girl friend sleep over when the children are visiting him.

13. Peter is concerned about Janet's drinking and leaving the children until late at night with baby sitters. Janet agrees to seek counseling regarding her drinking and to leave the children with Peter, if he is available, on nights when she will be out late.

14. Peter agrees to give Janet on a set basis such sums as she needs and are available from all common and outside sources, but not more than he can afford, given his own needs.

15. At the next meeting with the mediator, which is scheduled one week away, Peter will furnish Janet with all his sources of money and a list of his living expenses. Similarly, Janet will give Peter all of her sources of funds and a statement of her and the children's living expenses. At that meeting, they will attempt to reach an agreement regarding how much Peter will pay to Janet for support.

16. Both parents need time away from the children.

17. The parents agree that at this time the children will live with Janet, but will spend every Wednesday night and every other weekend with Peter.

18. Peter agrees not to ask for custody of the children at this time.

19. Nothing will be done about selling the home for at least six months from date, and Janet shall have the use of the home until it is sold. The parents will mediate the sale or retention of the home and the division of their equity at the next meeting.

Janet

Peter

Book Ordering

This book can be mail-ordered with a check or money order. The mail-order cost of one book is $12.00 plus $1.50 handling and mailing costs, or a total of $13.50. Please add $.50 for each additional book being mailed to the same address. For example, the cost of a two-book order is $24.00 and $2.00 shipping and handling costs.

Send payment and shipping instructions to:

Essential Publications
P.O. Box 101555
Birmingham, Alabama 35210

Volume discounts are available.

Communication With the Author

The author is available for consulting, interviews, general speaking engagements, and seminars for psychotherapists, divinity students, ministers, law students and lawyers. He may be reached by writing: Essential Publications, P.O. Box 101555, Birmingham, Alabama 35210. Please include your telephone number, time zone, and the best time in your time zone for him to return your call.